The Northumberland C

CW00487208

ITS CONCEPT ANE

With notes on the Central Northumberland Railway,
North Northumberland Railway,
South Northumberland Railway,
Scotswood & Scots Gap Railway
and
Killingworth & Scots Gap Railway

by

N.D.Mackichan

All proceeds to the Catherine Mackichan Trust
Scottish Registered Charity No: SC020459

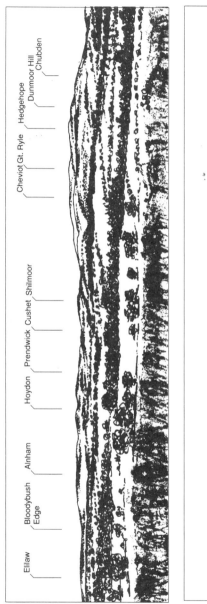

Eilaw Bloodybush Edge Alnham Hoydon Prendwick Cushet Shilmoor Cheviot Gt. Ryle Hedgehope Dunmoor Hill Chubden

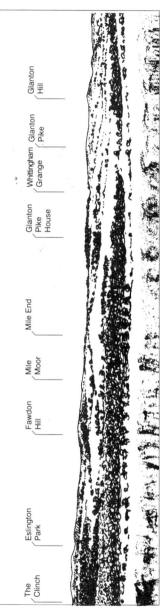

The Clinch Eslington Park Fawdon Hill Mile Moor Mile End Glanton Pike House Whittingham Grange Glanton Pike Glanton Hill

The North Side of the Vale of Whittingham as seen from the Callaly Road, near to Callaly Woods

Preface

The South Northumberland, Scotswood & Scots Gap, Killingworth & Scots Gap and North Northumberland Railway proposals are not well known or documented. This is hardly surprising in that, apart from never getting as far as track-laying or the ownership of locomotives or rolling stock, they were transient schemes and failed in the main for lack of financial support.

The history of the Northumberland Central Railway is a little different. To begin with, some 13 miles of track eventually were laid. Services were worked by hiring agreements with The North British Railway on behalf of the N.C.R between the years 1870 and 1872, after which, by an Act of Parliament, the Northumberland Central was absorbed into the North British system.

The Northumberland Central Railway therefore has a minor place in railway history, but it also has a place in legal history in that it was the first railway in Britain to utilise The Lands Improvement Co. as a means of raising finance. This caused problems and itself is therefore worthy of recording for posterity. But we must also see the Northumberland Central in the social and economic history of the county and indeed beyond the borders of Northumberland. Thus we are required to look at the other railway schemes listed earlier and consider the parts they were intended to or might have played.

The roles which some of the great estates of Central and North Northumberland played are crucial to our understanding of the chain of events. These differed and occasionally have been misinterpreted. Thus the role played by Sir John Swinburne over a lengthy lifetime changed from initial tremendous enthusiasm to a final withdrawal from the railway scene in 1880-81 when he realised the enormity of financial involvement required. The Ravensworths have been thought to be anti-railway but this was not always so. They were early supporters of The Stephensons and their lack of interest in some of the later railway promotions in Central Northumberland was less anti-railway landowners than shrewd financial assessors. The lack of enthusiasm of the Carr-Ellison family in the early period of our studies (1859-63) is harder to explain when set against their magnanimous gesture in 1864 and enthusiasm in later years (1880-81). At this stage it is often impossible to understand figures quoted (which indeed was a major contemporary complaint). Thus we quote the statements made by Sir Horace St Paul concerning the financial benefits which The Lands Improvement Scheme would make on his estate at Ewart Park. Reading these figures in 1998, they appear to be nothing less than impossible. But they were made, and to him must have seemed reasonable. We must leave their interpretation to the reader.

Beyond the bounds of Northumberland, influences were at work, for instance in the boroughs of Coldstream and Kelso. Finally the national economic situation had its effect, particularly the depression of 1866 which could hardly have come at a worse time for the struggling directors of the Northumberland Central Railway. The key part railway politics played, especially that of the great main line railways, The North Eastern, North British, Caledonian, Glasgow & South Western and Blyth & Tyne, and others further afield, are evident, even if after this length of time, this is open to a degree of interpretation.

Documentation of the Northumberland Central Railway is often less than satisfactory. This applies particularly to the finances. It was a constant cry at shareholders half-yearly meetings and elsewhere, particularly in the early days, that the accounts were presented in an unsatisfactory manner and often difficult to understand. If this was so a hundred and thirty years ago, we can hardly expect it to be any better now. The reader is warned, therefore, to take caution in interpreting figures. We have already quoted the case of Sir Horace St Paul and the Lands Improvement Co. benefits. There were more, and a mere selection of examples of complaints at shareholders meetings can be given.

In whatever form we view the Northumberland Central, we cannot escape the part played by the North Eastern and North British Railway, and of the latter company its chairman until 1866, Richard Hodgson of Carham. This figure, built perhaps in the mould of George Hudson, the Railway King, but on a lesser scale, still remains almost larger than life, with activities ranging from that of MP for Tynemouth, Chairman of The North British Railway, Director of The Northumberland Central, for which line he worked hard, Chairman of The River Tweed Commission and High Sheriff of Northumberland. His role in Northumberland Railway affairs is open to interpretation, but in the writer's view it seems impossible for a man of so many parts, of which we have only listed the highlights, to separate his activities into mentally watertight compartments. It is argued that they must have influenced each other, even if this is not the view held by at least one distinguished railway author. On these and other matters the reader must judge for himself.

One subject of continued debate connected with Richard Hodgson is the role in affairs played by the North British Railway. This leads us on to the motives of those promoting these lines. These cannot be resolved conclusively a century on, but the reader is asked to bear in mind two concepts. First is that of the "through-central route". This taxed many men's minds over many years and consisted of rival schemes for main lines geographically central in relation to the west coast and east coast routes between London, the English industrial conurbation's and the Forth-Clyde valley of Scotland. The best known, and most successful of these combined the Waverley Route of the North British and The Settle & Carlisle of the Midland. There were more and it can be argued with some force that the Northumberland Central was destined in some quarters to play a part in such a scenario. At the other end of the scale was the "local agricultural line", these being planned to serve perhaps one valley and its agricultural needs. Such lines would have the strong support of the owners of estates through which they passed. Between these extremes are some proposals which could be said to have aspects of both. For this reason, the full title of this work reads "The Northumberland Central Railway; Concept and Context".

The production of this work has only been possible with the assistance of many people. First, the late Father Nicholson of Whittingham encouraged the author to write an article (never published) for "Record & Recollections", the journal of the now sadly defunct Aln & Breamish Local History Society. Professor Norman McCord gave invaluable advice as to sources and layout. G.W.M Sewell, whose book "The North British Railway in Northumberland" (Merlin Books) is regarded as a model of accuracy gave unstintingly of his records and advice. Michael Oliver read the MSS and offered much sound advice. S.C Jenkins allowed me to quote from his work "The Rothbury Branch" (Oakwood Press), R.M Stevens of the Stephenson Locomotive Society discussed a number of points. My thanks must go to the staff of The Local Studies Department of the

Central Library of Newcastle upon Tyne, The Robinson Library of
The University of Newcastle upon Tyne and The Northumberland
and Scottish Record Offices. But as always, they cannot be held
responsible for errors which are all mine. Finally, technical help in
preparing final manuscript was given by George Skipper, of Alnwick.
The maps were prepared by John Rayner of Harbottle. John
Hutchinson drew the delightful illustrations and advised on the graphic
design and his wife, Val, undertook proof reading.

Chapter 1

The Broad Canvas

The Northumberland Central Railway has been largely ignored by railway historians. For example, The National Railway Museum could produce only one reference to the subject. This is a comparatively brief mention, dating back to 1917, within an article entitled "Rothbury and the Wansbeck and Northumberland Central Sections of the North British Railway"[1]. The reason for this is not hard to find. Whilst the history of the Northumberland Central Railway is a fascinating saga, with the possible exception of the Fontburn Viaduct this is not because of brilliant civil engineering features left in the landscape for posterity to admire. Similarly, the nostalgia of the railway buff will not be satisfied with memories of steaming monsters and gleaming carriages. At first sight, we are dealing with what appears to be more humdrum matters.

Among the tangle of threads which combine to make the story, we have the hopes and aspirations of well-intentioned individuals raised and dashed, enthusiastic amateurism sometimes amounting to plain incompetence, and professional railwaymen having to contend with this as best they may. All this was set amidst the railway politics of the Victorian era, in which the cut-and-thrust of powerful companies sent out shock-waves to affect the smaller fry in a variety of ways. The social history of some of the larger Northumberland estates has a key role to play. Economic history, not always noted for its compulsive reading, comes alive in crooked accountancy and disputed figures.

Any railway enterprise proposed, considered, partly created within other railway schemes, and re-submitted in one form or another over two decades, creates problems for the historian. This is certainly the case with The Northumberland Central. That the proposal was made at all indicates that a viable line existed in the minds of its promoters,(and indeed, its opponents) even if there were mixed motives involved. The N.C.R gestation period was inordinately protracted and the subsequent offspring something of a neutered dwarf; a mere shadow of the original intention. The sheer variety of subsequent attempts to rectify this means that, to say the least, all was not well. The causes were both national and local and, in considering those portions of the line which were built at later stages, we cannot assume that these materialised for the same reasons as were in the minds of the original speculators.

Thus, at the outset, we must place the Northumberland Central in its wider historical and geographical context. Of course we must consider that part which was constructed though not necessarily in detail, for this has been done elsewhere[2]. Rather, we must attempt to read into the minds of those early speculators, ponder on the politics of the large railway companies concerned, and study the management of some of the great landed estates of Northumberland. It is these factors which make the study of the Northumberland Central Railway so fascinating.

The early development of railways both to the north and south of the N.C.R arose out of the technological development of waggonways. With the exception of some primitive mining ventures in Europe, these were a peculiarly British invention[3]. This is of significance in the case of the N.C.R because to the south lay the great urban industrial region based around the rivers Tyne and Wear, within which territory many of the pioneers of railways had lived and worked. These collectively transformed the waggonways into railways in the modern sense[4]. These pioneers could not have operated without the financial backing of the aristocracy and landed gentry who, in many cases, were also coal-owners. Thus, an aristocracy who understood the advantages of the railway existed at an early date in Northumberland so that when, in time, the opportunity for rural railway development emerged, there existed those who were ready and willing to give their backing[5]. We can certainly see the relevance of the N.C.R in this context, but a better example is The Blyth and Tyne Railway. This line had its origins in some of the waggonways serving the South-East Northumberland Coalfield, which by processes of coalescence, expansion and technical improvement became a modern railway. As we shall see, it had a role to play in the affairs of the Northumberland Central which would have been crucial but for the fact that at the eleventh hour it was absorbed into the North Eastern Railway[6].

Similarly, though on a smaller scale, waggonway construction had been taking place in the coalfields north and south of the Firth of Forth. Of these perhaps the best known are The Fordell and The

Cockenzie, the latter immortalised because of its strategic prominence in the Battle of Prestonpans in 1745[7]. Whilst far ahead of the era in which the Northumberland Central Railway was conceived, these made for an early public awareness of the significance of railways. With a direct part to play in our story was the Edinburgh and Dalkeith, basically a mineral waggonway built to the Scottish standard gauge of 4' 6", on which progress had been made in various ways, principally by the carriage of passengers.[8]. An early liaison with the newly instituted North British Railway, centred on Edinburgh, followed by re-gauging and merger allowed for the expansion of the N.B.R southwards into the Central Borders, thus giving that railway the opportunity to promote alternative routes south other than by its east-coast line to Berwick. This was ultimately to form a successful part of the Mid-Britain, as opposed to East and West Coast trunk routes, a railway concept which produced many schemes of varying degrees of grandiose sophistication and practicality. As we shall see, this concept greatly affected the N.C.R.

The broad canvas required as an introduction has four urban, industrial areas at its periphery as is shown on the map pg12-13. The two most prominent were The North Eastern Railway based on Newcastle and The North British on Edinburgh. In Glasgow were based both The Caledonian and Glasgow & South Western Railways. The fourth corner was rather different, for here, in an area where the industrial revolution was certainly present but on a lesser scale and more widespread, no less than six major trunk routes eventually converged on Carlisle.(The Caledonian, Glasgow & South Western, London & North Western, Midland, North British and North Eastern). The North Eastern managed to swallow up the Newcastle & Carlisle Railway otherwise the latter might have had a much more prominent part to play, as will appear.

This map shows these and the intervening area, well known for its scenic grandeur of the Southern Uplands and Cheviot, Pennine and Galloway hills. These were intersected by long, sometimes deep and tortuous valleys, which, apart from a few localities like the Tweed Valley wool towns, supported only a sparse rural population.

A second map shows the railway situation in the North of England and Southern Scotland before the "The Railway Mania". This latter, occurring in the 1840's and early 1850's, before a period of industrial depression in the later years of that decade, arose from a state of euphoria concerning the new and revolutionary transport situation presented by the railways. Prior to that era, the waggonways were slowly beginning to be superseded by railways, the rapidly increasing efficiency of which was the result of technological progress. The railway of first concern to us is the Newcastle and Carlisle of 1836, though even this was a last minute replacement of a previously planned canal[9]. By 1839 thoughts were turned to the linking of the capitals of England and Scotland by rail, and to this was added the connection of Glasgow and a number of English cities. At this time at least four routes across The Border were under scrutiny, these being:

(i) An East Coast route from Newcastle via Berwick to Edinburgh. This had the advantage that routes to Newcastle from the south were already partially in existence or planned.

(ii) A Central route from Newcastle via Hexham, Jedburgh and Galashiels to Edinburgh. The advantage for this route lay in the fact that the Newcastle and Carlisle Railway was already open as far as Hexham.

(iii) A West coast route from Carlisle via Dumfries and Kilmarnock, and;

(iv) A West coast route from Carlisle via Annandale and Carstairs.

Of the west coast routes, the advantages for (iii) were that the gradients were easier and it could connect with the Glasgow, Paisley and Ayr Railway, already operating or under construction, but its mileage was greater and Edinburgh only reached by way of Glasgow. Route (iv) was much the most direct to both cities and could utilise local upgraded waggonways in the Clydesdale area, but its gradients were steeper and it avoided almost all the other towns of any size in Western Scotland. Both West coast routes had the advantage of being backed by the influential English Grand Union Railway, by whose tracks London would be reached. Both however had a formidable obstacle in the difficulties being experienced in building the Lancaster and Carlisle Railway through the Lune Gorge and over Shap Fell, which would bring access to Carlisle from the south.
In 1839 the government appointed a royal commission to

review the matter. The two expert commissioners were Lt-General Sir Frederick Smith and Professor Barlow. The Smith-Barlow Commission made two recommendations. If one route connecting England and Scotland were to be favoured then it should be the Annandale one but, if two were thought necessary, then the East Coast route should be the second one; in the event, no less than seven public railways were built across The Border [10].

Nationally the Railway Mania produced a plethora of proposed lines, in an age of enthusiasm and available capital investment but a scarcity of expertise. In general, these consisted of the remainder of the trunk routes, feeder lines and suburban networks to support these, and a number of often alternative competing routes between urban areas. These could be regarded as the "infill lines" of the railway map of Great Britain of which only a fraction came to fruition. This was for a variety of reasons, ranging from lack of finance or public support down to sheer impracticality. As part of this infill process, the railway map of Southern Scotland and Northern England, expanded in accordance with the expectations of the railway age, but railways came late to North and West Northumberland if one excludes the main lines (Edinburgh to Berwick in 1846 and Newcastle to Berwick in 1847). The Royal Border Bridge, connecting these two came later, as did the Sprouston branch of the N.E.R, due to connect with the N.B.R at Kelso, and the Alnwick branch, both completed in 1850. The Blyth and Tyne Railway Act came in 1852, but the basis of this company in upgraded colliery lines hardly achieved major railway status before its amalgamation into the N.E.R in 1874. 1852 also saw The Alston line becoming operational.

A combination of various circumstances accounted for this slow start. Most important was the terrain, as outlined above, where the marginal land of the hill country was only interspersed with pockets of good agricultural land, the exceptions being the Tweed valley and its tributaries, the hinterland of Alnwick and the lower North Tyne valley. There was a general expectation of mineral wealth in the area, of which there was just enough evidence to stimulate local and national interest. Lead mining south of the Tyne might have extended northwards, iron ore was found at Brinkburn and Bellingham. There were a few small coalpits and the possibility of a much larger coalfield centred on Plashetts together with good quarrying prospects including limestone for agricultural and building purposes. However, traffic was slow to build up, for much of this speculation ultimately turned out to be something of a myth.

A second reason for delay lay in the fact that the area fell between two major railway stools, these being the N.E.R and the N.B.R. In general, the former had astute management which meant that any promotion was likely to be well researched and fairly sure of success before being undertaken[11]. The latter was something of the opposite, where early expensive branch lines north of The Border, poor calibre management and inadequate supervision of sub-contractors caused financial restraints[12]. Both situations led to delay in developing branch lines south of The Border.

A final factor was the concept of a central mainline between the two countries. There were a number of failed attempts, most being countered by blocking tactics by rival companies. The only one to be successful was the already mentioned extension of the North British Hawick branch as the Border Union Railway, subsequently better known as the Waverley route, which reached Carlisle. This connected with the Midland Railway's Settle & Carlisle line. These projects costs both companies dear in both constructional and maintenance terms, and in operating expenses.

All these factors played a part in shaping The Northumberland Central Railway, most of which subsequent to the Northumberland Central Railway Act of 28th July 1863 existed only in the aspirations of its promoters. A second Act of Parliament, dated 2nd April 1867, allowed for abandonment of all the line except that between Scots Gap and Rothbury, opened to the public on 1st November 1870. This was worked from the outset by The North British Railway and the line was finally absorbed into that companies network by The Northumberland Central Railway and North British Railway Amalgamation Act of 1st February 1872(13). Thus the N.C.R fell into the N.B.R's net during the latter's expansionary efforts south of the Anglo-Scottish border and it is hard to see how even a start could have been made without the support and influence, though not capital investment, of that company, as will become apparent in the next chapter. Furthermore, this introduction of the N.C.R into the railway political arena did not stop at the Tyne and Forth, for other influences further north and south were at work.

In one other way the Northumberland Central had a place in

railway history. It was the scene of the first venture into railway development by The Lands Improvement Co the legality of which has been questioned (14). This alone ought to preserve the N.C.R from the near anonymity which was the fate of a number of other proposals with which it might have been linked. As it is, we are left with incomplete factual evidence which must be tempered with speculative interpretation of individual and corporate motives(15). The narrative requires the railway to be put into economic, social and industrial perspective. The "central area" around the Scots Gap to Rothbury portion as built had only modest traffic potential which could be anticipated, although some came too late to be of any help(16). The immediate contacts made at the boundaries of the railway produced the bulk of the traffic, whilst beyond this lay more distant but less certain traffic potential, prospects depending on how far on the one hand, local agricultural traffic developed and on the other how far the "through-route" schemes developed. These will be considered in subsequent chapters.

Chapter 2

The Origins

The Newcastle & Carlisle and The Newcastle & Berwick, were in existence in our area at the onset of our narrative. The N &.B.R was soon to become a part of the York, Newcastle & Berwick and, finally, of the North Eastern Railway. The N.E.R made an end-on junction immediately north of the Royal Border Bridge, and just south of Berwick station, with the North British Railway to produce a through east-coast route connecting London and Edinburgh. Both the N.B.R and the N.E.R had by 1850 begun to serve the rich agricultural Tweed valley. The N.B.R had begun branches in Southern Scotland but had not yet reached the potentially lucrative markets in the woollen mill areas around Galashiels. One branch had however reached Kelso and ultimately connected with the N.E.R branch from Tweedmouth to Sprouston.

In Northumberland, the York, Newcastle & Berwick Railway of 1845, favoured by Stephenson, was the final route chosen from a number of proposals from 1835 onwards, to make this all-important east coast connection. Details of these need not concern us, except to say that, whether promoted from north or south of The Border, all but two adopted alignments near the coast(1).

The two exceptions require a brief comment. A proposal made in 1840, but never formally presented to parliament, was basically a deviation from the Stephenson route to include Morpeth (2). We shall see presently something of the critical role in developments played by the lobbies of the ancient county towns of Northumberland (Some citizens of Alnwick, for example, never forgave the Newcastle & Berwick for placing their town at the end of a branch). The other route, at first sight a strange one, was proposed in 1839 by The Edinburgh & Dalkeith Railway. This was for a Newcastle extension, being a line from Dalkeith via Coldstream, Wooler, Whittingham and Longhorsley to Newcastle, roughly following the line of the turnpike road (the modern A68 and A697). This scheme had its roots in a proposal of 1817 for a Kelso, Melrose and Dalkeith waggonway. In 1820 the survey was completed by Robert Stephenson of Glasgow (no connection with the more famous Tyneside railway pioneer of the same name). Remarkably, and in sharp contrast to later railway investment in the area, the £55,000 capital required was raised within one month. In spite of this, the scheme did not go ahead. It was resurrected in 1838 and re-surveyed by Rennie. Today, we would agree with Bowman, a Morpeth engineer, that the gradients of the Dalkeith extension would prove too severe, (though it was to him that we owe the infamous Morpeth curve). Bowman dismissed Rennie's line as "too hilly", but concluded that it would make "a good branch line"(3). Indeed, these remarks would apply to a railway in the modern concept, but The Edinburgh & Dalkeith was at that time merely an enlarged and metamorphosing waggonway of Scottish standard gauge (4' 6"). It was not therefore compatible with the gauge of the developing East Coast trunk route. The gradients were acceptable within the confines of the wagonway era, in which, for example, stationary engines with winding gear were still the accepted norm(4).

Our interest in the above proposal is twofold. First is the fact that The Edinburgh & Dalkeith was, at that time, within one year of formal merger proposals with the N.B.R and was even then making overtures to that company for joint working, necessitating its re-gauging to achieve compatibility. This quickly led to the idea of expansion through The Borders to Galashiels, Carlisle and England. Were the directors and others with N.B.R interests at heart already looking to an independent access to Newcastle and the South? Secondly, do we have a clear demonstration, at this early stage, before the Railway Mania was in full cry, that some influential people were already looking specifically towards that area which was to become the province of the Northumberland Central Railway? This should be borne in mind when we come to consider other proposed routes in the valleys of the Coquet, Aln, Till, Glen and Tweed in later chapters.

After the opening of the Newcastle & Berwick Railway in July 1847, George Hudson, "The Railway King", had his sights set on obtaining control of the North British Railway, then in a weak financial state. The latter's position rose principally from the too rapid proliferation of branch lines, with the air of optimism prevalent at the time suggesting higher returns than were realised.(a situation by no means unique to the North British),and damage caused by the flooding of unconsolidated earthworks on the main line in the summer of 1846, which proved expensive to repair. Hudson would then have

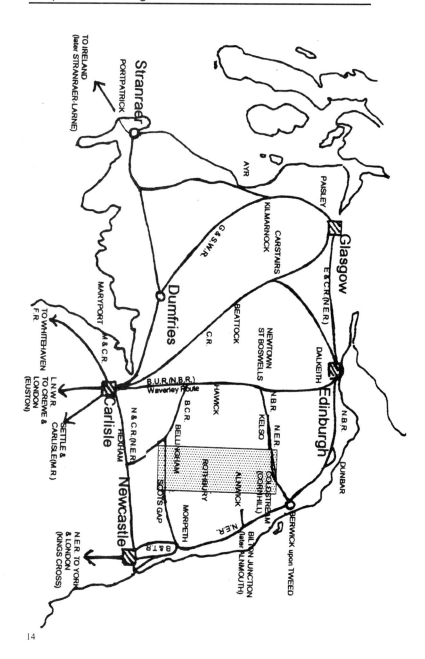

Diagram of Major Railway Network of Northern England and
Southern Scotland, within which the Northumberland Central
Railway was set. (Minor routes not shown)

The four major urban/industrial areas are shown

Main Area of Northumberland Central Railway shown

Railways later absorbing another company shown in brackets
eg N & CR (N.E.R)

B.C.R	Border Counties Railway (N.B.R)
B.U.R	Border Union Railway (N.B.R)
B & T.R	Blyth & Tyne Railway
C.R	Caledonian Railway
E & G.R	Edinburgh & Glasgow Railway (N.B.R)
F.R	Furness Railway
G & S.W.R	Glasgow & South Western Railway
L & N.W.R	London & North Western Railway
M.R	Midland Railway
M & C.R	Maryport & Carlisle Railway
N.B.R	North British Railway
N & C.R	Newcastle & Carlisle Railway
N.E.R	North Eastern Railway
W.R	Wansbeck Railway

had control of a continuous route from Rugby to Edinburgh, and after swallowing up The Edinburgh & Glasgow Railway, to the latter city as well. Protracted negotiations took place between Messrs Philipson and Alheusen of Newcastle, and Wotherspoon of Liverpool (an N.B.R shareholder) on behalf of Hudson and Learmonth, Chairman of the N.B.R. Stalling tactics enabled Learmonth to ride the storm until a brief financial respite came(5).

Hudson's failure to press home his predatory attack arose partially from threats to his rear. The Leeds & Thirsk Railway was dissatisfied with traffic arrangements with the Hudson group of railway companies. They sought a route north of Leeds independent of Hudson. In collaboration with this would have come the proposed Newcastle, Edinburgh and Direct Glasgow Railway, a Northumberland initiative but doubtless with the activities of The Leeds & Thirsk in mind. The N.E.& D.G.R would have been a 'central' route from Newcastle via Ponteland, Otterburn, Redesdale and Jedburgh(6). Success for either party would have sealed the fate of the Northumberland Central one way or the other.

In 1845-6, a group of Newcastle railway speculators backed by the Newcastle Journal attempted to persuade Hudson to leave the N.B.R to its fate. The basic tenets of their arguments were that the N.B.R would require £100,000 for necessary repairs and as much again to put it on a sound financial footing. This was only a little less than the cost of a Hudson promoted independent route to Edinburgh. The Newcastle Journal stated "[that] the Tweed Valley would be ideal for a line independent of the North British to Edinburgh". Doubtless this statement arose from the fact that in 1845 the N.B.R surveyed a branch from St Boswells via Roxburgh and Kelso to unite "with a line from the Berwick direction". This appears more than an empty gesture because the directors of the Newcastle & Berwick Railway met on 19th November 1846 for the purpose of letting the contract for the Border Bridge. The Newcastle Journal reported a suggestion at this meeting of a more direct line than the N.B.R's, crossing the Tweed about ten miles higher up, which at much less cost would form a junction with the Newcastle and Berwick's existing Kelso branch. The Newcastle Journal followed this with strong support for Hudson, including his possible take-over bid "....*the offer made by Mr Hudson appears to be an extremely liberal one, and by no means indicative of a desire to obtain the line cheap. We are certain it is much more than the Company can reasonably hope to realise by an independent management. With a competing line to Edinburgh joining the Newcastle & Berwick, the difficulties for the North British would be seriously increased. Such a line, as we have already said, is contemplated; and, in view thereof the contracts for building the bridge over the Tweed have been suspended. Preparations are making [sic] for the survey of a line which will leave the Newcastle & Berwick line at a point near Belford, pass Twizel, Coldstream and Greenlaw, through a rich agricultural country to Edinburgh, and though some extensive works will be required upon it, they are not, we are assured, of a character that will present the slightest engineering difficulty, and the route will be much shorter(7)".*

Whilst nothing came of this proposal, in any case perhaps nothing more than a tactical move, it may have emphasised to the directors of the N.B.R the weakness of their southern flank, thereby influencing them to form policies which supported proposals along the lines of the Northumberland Central.

At first sight, West-coast railway developments would seem to have little influence on the promotion of lines in the territory of The Northumberland Central, but this was possibly not the case. The Smith-Barlow recommendations favouring the Annandale route were delayed until 1841 and the main line, now to become The Caledonian Railway, was not opened until 14th February 1848. However, this completed a continuous rail link between London and Glasgow, some two and a half years ahead of the East-coast line which was delayed by the building of the Tyne and Border bridges.

Prior to its completion, The Caledonian Board had been asked to attend a London meeting convened to negotiate the sharing of Anglo-Scottish traffic. This was chaired by Captain Mark Huish of The London & North Western Railway, the west coast partner of the Caledonian, but in spite of this, the Caledonian declined to attend. The proposal of concern here related to the division of goods traffic so as to prevent a price war. It was suggested that traffic from London and places west of Halifax should go via the west coast route and traffic east of Leicester and Halifax via the east coast. There would be no arbitrary division of traffic to the north of Edinburgh and Glasgow. The Caledonian had its own reasons for not attending. It was playing a lone hand, having set its sights on as much of the developing traffic north of the Forth-Clyde valley as possible. Indeed, there was deadlock at a further meeting at which the Caledonian was represented(8).

All this made the weakened North British even more suspicious of events to the south, particularly when in 1846 the Caledonian proposed a branch to join the Newcastle & Carlisle at Brampton, a revival of an old waggonway scheme of 1825. The motive behind this was to filter off east coast, and specifically Newcastle traffic to Glasgow and Edinburgh, via the west coast route. The C.R Board would, in fact, have liked to absorb the N & C.R into its system which would have opened a variety of options for expansion. However, in 1846 the Caledonian finances were also depleted, and for the same reasons as the North British, promoting too many branch lines at the same time as the completion of the main line was exceeding its budget. This meant that there was no available cash to invest in the Edinburgh & Glasgow Railway, again a scheme which would have opened the door to various Scottish projects. The E & G.R was certainly up for grabs because of an absurd price war with the competing canals, which was driving it to bankruptcy. This prize eventually fell to the N.B.R(9).

Also in 1846, John Hodgson-Hinde, M.P for Newcastle, Chairman of the Newcastle & Carlisle and a director of The Caledonian, was about to retire. Before relinquishing office, he tried to force through a merger between these companies. The Caledonian, as stated above, was in no position to complete what would have amounted to a take-over. If this had been accomplished, the enlarged Caledonian would have blocked all "central" north-south routes with consequences in north and west Northumberland. Thus, the N.B.R could have been prevented from completing The Waverley route (Edinburgh-Carlisle, in one of several forms, all much disputed). More certainly, The Border Counties Railway soon to become a N.B.R branch, would have been in difficulties. If the N.B.R continued with its obsession in obtaining an independent route south of The Border, then the agreement with the North Eastern Railway concerning running powers to Newcastle or elsewhere (see below) would have stood little chance of becoming operational, in which case the upgrading of the N.C.R into a major line might have occurred (10).

1845 saw yet another Caledonian threat in a remarkable proposal, The Caledonian Extension Railway. This was for a line from Ayr via The Tweed valley to Berwick, based on an old waggonway scheme of 1807. The civil engineer involved was again Rennie and his scheme to link the ports of Glasgow and Berwick was not formally abandoned until 1838, only to be revived and modified by the Caledonian Board seven years later. This may well have been an empty threat because, if forced to implement it, it is difficult to see how the Caledonian would have coped financially. What this costly venture would have done is to cut across all routes south from Central Scotland, including any proposals by the rival North British and Glasgow, Dumfries and Carlisle Railways, of which the latter had much popular support in Glasgow(11). The N.B.R responded with a proposed line west from Peebles through the Biggar gap, regarded by Mullay as "an empty threat"(12). However, this may not be the case, in that the independent Symington, Biggar and Broughton Railway now moved into the Caledonian camp, with which it was connected at Symington, pledging that if the proposed Galashiels, Innerleithen and Peebles line (N.B.R backed) were to be defeated that it would build to Galashiels. This would have opened up the whole Tweed valley area to the Caledonian Railway as previously implied by the Caledonian Extension Railway. Whilst Caledonian influences were at work, there was an absence of Caledonian cash and, with its heavy commitments to the Forth-Clyde valley area, it is hard to see much prospect of financial support until after the recession. We shall meet up with this situation again in Chapter 11 in a later and somewhat modified guise.

In the end, the N.B.R counter plan to the above might not have been such an empty threat. Richard Hodgson, as Chairman of the N.B.R, moved in when the act was defeated "to preserve the proper right of the N.B.R to the district" acting on this with a new proposal for an N.B.R Act of June 1861 which gave the N.B.R access to Innerleithin in 1864 and Galashiels two years later. We shall meet the formidable Richard Hodgson again in connection with the Northumberland Central.

This brings us to events relating to the "central" routes between England and Scotland, something of a misnomer, as will become apparent but one hallowed by time and convention. Many ideas were floated around, some wildly optimistic, others purely political blocking tactics with no intention of being built. A small number had a real chance of success. Of these one or two might have affected the territory of the Northumberland Central and thus require brief consideration.

First, we may consider a very successful line, The Stainmore route; a complicated saga in itself arising from the need to transport hematite from Cumbria to Tees-side and in the reverse direction coking coal from Durham. The principal component company was the South Durham & Lancashire Union Railway, backed by the London & North Western and Stockton & Darlington Railways. The final route chosen was a compromise with rival unsuccessful schemes e.g. The York & Carlisle Railway of 1845 and the York & Glasgow Union (from south-east to north-west) and the Liverpool, Manchester and Newcastle Junction combining with the Lancs & North Yorkshire Railway of 1846 (from south-west to north-east). For our purposes, the outcome of these rival schemes was the Stainmore and Eden Valley Railway, serving as something of a cross-country block to most central expansionist schemes, the potential exceptions being via either the Eden or Derwent valleys.

North of the Tyne and to the west of the coastal plain, two main valleys, the North Tyne and Rede, could be exploited for rail purposes. Both had their protagonists. First in the field was the Tyne & Edinburgh promoted in 1835 and appearing in a circular by Stephenson Reed of Newcastle, inviting subscriptions towards a survey(13). The plan was for a junction with the Newcastle & Carlisle at Warden, near Hexham, thence up the North Tyne and Rede valleys to a tunnel at Carter Fell, and thence via Jedburgh to Edinburgh. This was followed in the next year by The Newcastle, Edinburgh & Glasgow Railway, which was to run directly from Newcastle to Otterburn and then to follow the Tyne & Edinburgh route with a branch to Glasgow. A number of other somewhat similar proposals continued to be made right down to the Manchester, Hawick and Glasgow Direct Railway of 1892, of possible significance, as will be outlined in Chapter 11.

Similarly, a number of proposals were put forward utilising the North Tyne route, beginning with the Hexham, Kielder and Galashiels to Edinburgh. Of greater significance was a N & C.R scheme of 1845 for a line from its Bellingham branch northwards into Scotland, as above, together with a link southwards via the Wear Valley Railway. How far this had the long-term prospect of becoming a central route is difficult to assess. It seems connected with the anti-Hudson lobby building up in places like York and London, and may have had more political than transport significance(14).

The route which did succeed was The Border Counties Railway which eventually made a connection via its Liddesdale extension with The Border Union Railway, promoted as an extension of the Galashiels branch of the N.B.R. This reached The Border at Carlisle in the face of fierce opposition from the Caledonian, and at enormous expense, to make a through route to the south via the London & North Western, to Ireland via The Glasgow & South Western and North Channel ferries and, ultimately London via a true "central" route, The Midland's Settle & Carlisle line. The L & N.W.R connection was not actively pursued, surprisingly, because of the railway political situation, in which the N.B.R did not want to invoke the wrath of the mighty George Hudson, "The Railway King", by any suggestion of diverting traffic away from the east to west coast route. We shall return to this theme later.

Finally two further "central" openings to the south remained available to the North British directors. One of these, to the east, was one of several possibilities of exploiting co-operation with The Blyth & Tyne Railway. It involved the building of a new bridge over The Tyne downstream from Newcastle and thence via the West Hartlepool Railway (which had L.& N.W. backing) to reach the still independent Stockton & Darlington Railway and from there south by one of several routes. North of B & T.R territory this line might have been expected to enter Northumberland Central territory. A second way of exploiting the B & T.R connection was via The Wansbeck Railway,(The Wanney Line") promoted and built to connect the Border Counties with the Blyth & Tyne at Morpeth. This played a significant role and will be considered in the next chapter.

The final possibility utilised the Derwent Valley gap south of the Tyne. Tomlinson(15) quotes the evidence for the Newcastle, Derwent and Weardale Junction Railway promoted in 1859, briskly countered by a North Eastern Railway bill for a branch line to Blaydon, Consett and the Lanchester valley. Loss of the Derwent valley to a rival company, such as the N.D.& W.J.R could have allowed the

L.&.N.W.R access into Newcastle. The defection to the North Eastern camp of the Stockton & Darlington Railway meant they would be unable to co-operate with the Derwent Valley Railway, and caused these schemes to elapse.

And so we come to the remaining route north-south, that exploiting the Coquet Valley and the valleys of the Aln, Breamish, Glen and Beaumont. At last, we are into the territory of the Northumberland Central Railway. In the next chapter we shall consider the local scene.

Skew Bridge

Chapter 3

The Local Scene

The first two chapters have allowed us to place the embryonic Northumberland Central Railway in its context. To sum up, this consists of east, west and possible central main lines between the two railway powerbases of Edinburgh and Newcastle (and to some extent other centres such as Glasgow and Leeds). We have noted that between the industrial areas centred on these cities, the rural Borders were sparsely populated There were areas of good low-lying agricultural land which would certainly benefit from rail links, but few towns of even modest size. The uplands were marginal land at best, intersected by deep valleys, presenting severe problems in both financial and constructional terms to the railway developers. At the onset of the railway mania, traditionally dated to 1844, infill railway construction had hardly begun even in the low-lying agricultural districts of Northumberland, territory which might be expected to prove easier in building terms, and from which the anticipated return on capital invested might be more rewarding.

The year 1852 saw the first tentative effort to promote railways in the Coquet valley. The Acklington and Rothbury Railway was a logical extension of the 1852 Tynemouth Dock, Morpeth and Shields Direct Railway(1). Thomas Riddell was chairman of the committee promoting this early venture and the line was to run via Felton and Weldon Bridge. Although the promoters of this route failed in their objective, two developments were the outcome. One was local stimulation of individuals to consider railway routes to the north and west, whilst the other was the forcing of the Blyth and Tyne Railway to promote its own outlet to Morpeth. This had unanticipated consequences as will appear presently.

The next promotion followed a year later when a committee including such landowners as Sir Walter Trevelyan, A.R.Fenwick (of the Earl of Carlisle's Northumberland estates) and W.H.Cadogan of Brinkburn promoted a more ambitious scheme. This was for an initial branch from Morpeth to Rothbury at an estimated cost of £80,000. The location of ironstone at Brinkburn held the prospect that if coal could be economically transported to the site, that an ironworks would become viable (This in fact occurred in 1856, but the hoped for iron resources were unsatisfactory and the venture proved short-lived). Lime was needed generally for the new methods of modern agriculture and Trevelyan hoped to exploit limestone in his territory. It was also needed for construction work in Morpeth and the rapidly expanding industrial area of the south-east of the county. The Rothbury & Acklington Railway Incorporated Co. (for railway and construction purposes) dates from the 3rd November 1853, proposing a Bill in the next session of parliament. The cost was put at only £5,000 per mile, in spite of the need for two viaducts. The scheme envisaged working arrangements with the York, Newcastle & Berwick Railway at Acklington. The route was to run via Warkworth (presumably for harbour facilities), Acklington, West Chevington, Eshott, Felton, Brinkburn (South Side), Brinkburn (High Wood), Pauperhaugh, Raw Leeward, Hesleyhurst, Hollingshill, Mounthealey and Whitton to a terminus at Rothbury. However, interest, presumably with a touch of novelty, was such that the scheme was extended beyond Rothbury to Whittingham, Wooler and Maxwellhaugh (Kelso) That this was a serious undertaking is indicated by the fact that Lock and Errington were engaged as surveyors, at a time when they were great names in a new speciality where skills were scarce and commanded an appropriate price. The route was ultimately changed as the original plan "would merely be a valley route inland from the coast". What was felt to be required was "a route across the valleys, from Morpeth via Netherwitton, Rothbury, and Whittingham to Wooler and therefrom via the Beaumont and Kail Waters to Old Roxburgh to unite with the North British" The provisional survey report by Errington indicated that "(the line) could be constructed with easy gradients without a single difficult work" and his plan shows the route as being from Morpeth (Stobhill Junction), thence through Mitford, Melton, Hartburn, Longwitton, Roughlees, Forestburn, and so to Brinkburn and Rothbury, south of the Coquet. Goods traffic was described in the prospectus as building stone, limestone, clay, "abundant ironstone", cereals, mixed goods, manures, timber, slates, tar oil, sheep, pigs, cattle etc. A London Co. had been formed for working ironstone at Brinkburn, with an estimate of 150 tons per week. So confident were the promoters that they forecast a population explosion in the Coquet Valley of about 700!

Surprisingly, once again, nothing came of this scheme even though it had the merit of connections with two main lines, which, even if not then complete, could have been expected to engender through traffic. Lack of interest by either major company is surprising in view of later events and one is left to conclude that the scheme was ahead of its time(2). One point of note is that two firms of solicitors were given, these being Thorp and Dickson of Alnwick and Woodman, whose offices were in Morpeth. The former must indicate some form of Alnwick connection. We shall meet the latter frequently. This intrepid railway legal expert and company secretary appears often in the unfolding saga.

At the same time, important neighbouring developments were afoot. The York & North Midland, Leeds Northern and York Newcastle & Berwick amalgamated on 31st.July 1854 to become the North Eastern Railway. The Newcastle & Carlisle Railway had considered a branch to Bellingham to bring cheaper coal to the ironworks there, which from 1841 were operating at a loss, or, alternatively to exploit the local coalfield based on Plashetts, then thought to be extensive, for this purpose. It also backed a Carter Bar scheme for a central route to Scotland where Plashetts coal might have been expected to be cheaper than that from Lanarkshire for the woollen mills north of the Border. The Border Union Railway was then under active promotion. In October 1844 the North British Railway Board, having reached the Galashiels area from its extension of the Edinburgh and Dalkeith, considered a projection to Carlisle but rejected this, deciding against a minority board view to build to Hawick. It also dropped a scheme to build a line from Berwick to Kelso (which if built might have been one logical northern extension of the N.C.R). It did, however, invite the Glasgow, Dumfries and Carlisle Railway to create a joint trunk route from Carlisle to Edinburgh. Mullay quotes the economic historian C.J.A.Robertson as believing that the N.B.R was willing to leave the route south of Hawick to another company (say, the G,D & C.R via the Esk valley) whose chance of a successful promotion against the might of the Caledonian Railway was at best doubtful. This indicates that the N.B.R at this stage did not attach high priority to the Carlisle line as a through route, a view which was going to change radically(3). However, in view of the N.B.R finances at the time, and with even its main line to Berwick not scheduled to commence operations until 1846, it seems more likely that the directors dare not face the shareholders with further extravagant construction plans, before a single mile of revenue-earning track was in operation.

However, all the evidence points to continuing N.B.R plans for expansion south of the Border. It was not the profit from transporting Plashett's coal alone which interested the directors of the N.B.R and in particular, its ambitious chairman, Richard Hodgson, who lived at Carham in North Northumberland. He and his directors promoted good relationships with the Newcastle & Carlisle with a view to potential outlets southwards independent of the North Eastern Railway. The Railway Times of 20th.February 1858 stated *"[the N.B.Co] must either submit to be expunged from the political railway map of the country, and sink down into a mere dependent of the N.E.R whilst the Caledonian Railway with its southern and northern alliances rides rough-shod over its east coast competitor, or [the North British] must establish for itself outlets that can be felt even in the centre of England"*

Hodgson acted, and with the methods the N.B.R had used on previous occasions by backing an independently constructed branch line and when this was complete, buying it out. This time, however, it was on the grand scale. The Border Counties Railway Act (North Tyne Section) was passed on 31st July 1854. As Sewell say, the very wording of the Act meant that from the start, other sections were intended(4). The initial meeting of the proposers led by W.H Charlton of Hesleyside, unquestionably supported by his friend Hodgson amongst other interested parties, took place in March 1854 at the Furnace Inn, Bellingham. Charlton of Hesleyside in the North Tyne Valley was elected Chairman of the Board of Directors. Others, involved at an early stage (in fact as far back as the previous year) were "The London Connection including engineers and parliamentary agents" T.J Taylor of Bellingham, the agent of the Duke of Northumberland, The Hareshaw Ironworks at Bellingham and the mortgagee, The Union Bank, J.F Tone, whom we shall meet later, the lessee of Plashetts mine, was also the B.C.R civil engineer and a major shareholder(5). Hodgson's support for a central route south, fitting in with this new promotion, took the form of co-operation with the Hexham, Darlington and Hartlepool promotion of 1859. This, though abortive, shows Hodgson's aggressive interests in southern extensions, of which there were others, for example the Hexham and Skipton proposal of 1862(6).

The first sod of the Border Counties Railway was cut on 11th December 1855 and work proceeded in stages. Two further Acts

(The Border Counties Railway (Liddesdale Diversion) of 1859 and The North British & Border Counties Railway Amalgamation Act of 13th.August 1860), completed both the building of the line and its rapid absorption into the North British Railway. The important point here was that the junction with the Border Union Railway (Waverley route of the N.B.R) effectively sealed off other railway routes to the west (7)

With the railway mania now beginning to see results nationally, interest in east-west and central Northumberland routes grew. There is no doubt that the catalyst for the Wansbeck Railway was progress on the Border Counties, as outlined above. We have seen that W.H Cadogen, believing that his Brinkburn estate could viably produce coal, iron and limestone, was attempting to interest his neighbouring landowners in branch-line developments. A further attempt along the lines of the scheme outlined above was made in 1855. This was locally inspired and planned to connect Morpeth with Rothbury via Meldon, Hartburn and Longwitton. Although surveyed by Willett, the proposal came to nothing(8). At this stage, the prospectus was issued under the names of landowners such as Cadogan, Trevelyan and Fenwick, but there is little doubt that matters were being watched by Richard Hodgson, ever with an eye to an opportunity, as chairman of the North British Railway. It can hardly be coincidental that The Border Counties Railway Act of 1859 increased the authorised capital at a time when the B.C.R shares were not being taken up in full and that this vacuum was filled by North British injection of capital and board membership(9).

The result was the Wansbeck Railway Act of 8th.July 1859. This was significantly successful when previous schemes had failed e.g. a revival of the Acklington branch plan, and a proposed extension of the Alnwick branch of the North Eastern Railway(10). The line would link The Border Counties (soon to become part of the N.B.R.) with the Morpeth extension of the Blyth and Tyne Railway. The success of the Wansbeck line over the others lay in the power behind the throne of Hodgson and the N.B.R. Hodgson maintained stoutly that he acted purely independently, in a period of rapid railway expansion and much railway diplomatic activity, it is hard to justify this stance as anything more than rhetoric in the "he that protesteth" vein. Warn (11) actually states that the N.B.R steered the W.V.R Act through parliament but the hard evidence for this is lacking. However,

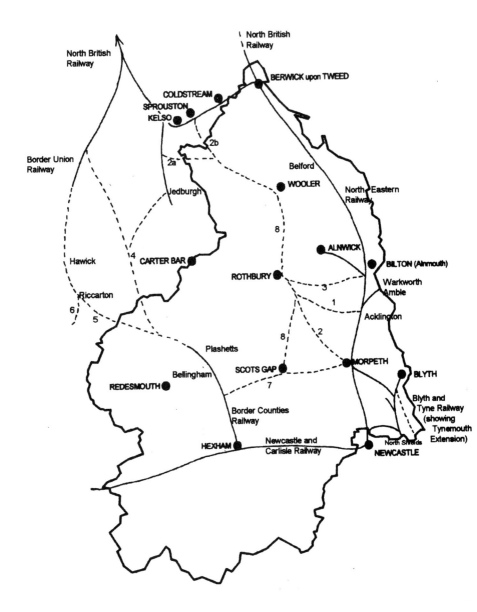

Mid and North Northumberland Proposed Railway
Developments 1856 - 59

1	Rothbury and Acklington Railway 1852 (et sub)
2	Morpeth, Rothbury and Maxwellhaugh Railway 1854 (with variants 2a and2b)
3	Rothbury and Alnwick Railway 1856
4	Teviotdale Railway (B.C.R) 1856
5	Liddesdale Extension (B.C.R) 1859
6	Hawick - Carlisle Extension (B.U.R)
7	Wansbeck Valley Railway 1859
8	Northumberland Central Railway 1856 - 62 (Existing railways shown in continuous line) (Scemes proposed prior to 1856 not shown)

Hodgson appears to have guaranteed Trevelyan 50% of the capital from N.B.R sources if the bill were successful(12). There seems to be an ambivalence amongst the attitudes of the principal promoters. Thus, Trevelyan, stated that the advantage of the railway was to the district rather than to national shareholders, yet waxed lyrical about the connection with the great railway systems of the east and west, the ports of Northumberland, Cumberland and Southern Scotland and, significantly the manufacturers of Southern Scotland(13). Perhaps he spoke with one voice to those living in the district and another to Hodgson and the Board of the N.B.R. However even the Act recognised the W.R as a through route, allowing the N.B.R and the B,& T.R to contribute £50,000 of capital each and appointing a director to the board of the W.R if they took up this injection of capital. The inevitable followed, a slow start, and various difficulties but Benjamin Woodman, whom we have already met in his capacity of secretary, was able to announce at the February 1862 meeting that Scots Gap to Morpeth was nearly ready for opening(14). Whilst the revenue from the first six months of traffic between Morpeth and Scots Gap showed a small profit, there was a loss on the capital account. The N.B.R (Wansbeck & Finances Act) including the absorption of the W.R was granted in July 1863 before stages 2 and 3 of the W.R had been completed i.e. at a time when there was no physical connection at Reedsmouth with the N.B.R Border Counties branch, as it had now become!(15). Indeed, we now see a firm east-west coalition building up to counter Caledonian and North-Eastern Railway interests, consisting of the Furness, Maryport & Carlisle, North British and Blyth & Tyne Railways, the latter working some if not all of the N.B.R Wansbeck Valley Branch, as it had become, until the physical connection at Reedsmouth had been made.

    1862 saw other important developments in The Borders. On the 8th July it was announced that the Border Union had an opening timetable. It was now called The Waverley Route and the timetable referring to the B.U.R and B.C.R stated *"(it was) the only direct route from England for the whole of the South, East and West Coasts (of Scotland), and from Edinburgh into the Historic Borders"*. Prior to this, the half yearly meeting of the Blyth and Tyne Railway held at its Newcastle Headquarters with Joseph Laycock in the chair, recommended adoption of the chairman's report that "the last six months were mostly routine and of a quiet nature". This was rather typical of the B & T.R because in fact it had obtained an Act for a branch line to Walbottle Colliery; "(it) might seem to people not well acquainted with traffic .... that line would be through a district which would scarcely admit of carrying a line through. But they had arrangements with a very extensive colliery that would secure the company a remunerative return if the particular branch was made. The B & T Board knew what it was doing because the preference share dividend declared was 10% and 9.5% on ordinary. But even the B & T Board might have failed to see the consequences still far in the future(16).

1862 also saw an important phase in railway infighting come to a close, when the Newcastle & Carlisle was taken over by the N.E.R. Attempts to gain control of the N & C.R have already received mention as first occurring in April 1848 when the Chairman of that company was about to retire. John Hodgson-Hinde, M.P for Newcastle, director of the Caledonian Railway and the half brother of Richard Hodgson of the North British Railway, saw that Hudson was not in a position to take the N & C.R into his empire which was financially stretched, so he attempted to drum up support for a Caledonian take-over. This proved also impossible and for the same reasons. Finally with the absorption of the Border Counties into the N.B.R, the directors of the North Eastern saw a threat of penetration into Newcastle, and beat this off by making an offer to the N & C.R which was accepted. Hodgson was thus beaten tactically but this allowed him to develop *"a clever strategy"... "to obtain an independent access to Newcastle via the Blyth & Tyne... the Wansbeck Valley railway being obviously promoted to complete a new route between Morpeth and Edinburgh which would enable the N.B.R to coerce the N.E.R into paying them a larger proportion of the joint revenue or offering better terms of amalgamation."* (17). The N.B.R had obtained access to Newcastle via the Border Counties and Newcastle & Carlisle (see below). In reporting this the Newcastle Daily Chronicle of August 11th 1862 protested about the working arrangements which did not allow the N.B.R to stop between Hexham and Newcastle, but this must be seen an a sensible clause written in by the N.E.R in order to protect its income from traffic on that line. It was quickly rescinded as a result of protests.

The most far-reaching event in 1862 as regards the future success of the Northumberland Central Railway was without doubt the well known but controversial agreement between the North British and North Eastern Railways. This did not come into effect until 1869 but from the outset its implications were dramatic. The agreement allowed the N.E.R running powers from Berwick to Edinburgh (and indeed north onto the Scottish Central and other lines but these options were never taken up). In exchange the North British obtained running powers into Newcastle via the Border Counties and Hexham. The well-known 19th century railway recorder E.L Ahrons, in an oft-quoted remark said that the *"North British had sold its birthright for a mess of pottage"*. In a superficial sense this was right in that N.E.R express trains could proceed from Newcastle to Edinburgh under these running powers, whilst the N.B.R had to run by The Border Counties Branch and the Newcastle and Carlisle, now a part of the N.E.R The distance between Edinburgh and Newcastle via Riccarton (128.5 miles) is only four miles longer than via Berwick, but the Border Counties was in no sense an alternative main line — "the ruling gradient of 1:100 occurs with a frequency that makes the ascent of the valley of the North Tyne a toilsome journey" (18).— and that is only the beginning for further ahead lay Whitrope and Falahill summits on the Waverley route. Be that as it may, it has often been said that if the Border Counties Railway had been built to the high-speed specifications of the Settle and Carlisle, running through not dissimilar territory, that a central main line could have proved viable e.g. with The Great North of England as described by Mulley(19).

The Ahrons misconception is that the 57 miles of, admittedly, main line between Berwick and Edinburgh was essential to the finances of the N.B.R On this line, it retained goods traffic under its control, and it is an old axiom that prestige came from the smart 4-4-0's hauling fine express trains but the profits were made by the humble 0-6-0's on the goods trains. The N.B.R directors merely regarded the running powers of the N.E.R to Edinburgh as the hiring of trains, a not uncommon practice. This made sense both with regard to the notoriously parlous state of N.B.R locomotive resources at the time and the logistics of having locos and crews bound up in transferring east coast expresses at Berwick for the last 57 miles. Furthermore, and a subject which need only briefly be mentioned here, the N.B.R revenues came from the absorbed Edinburgh & Glasgow main line, snatched from the jaws of the Caledonian Railway, and the coal traffic of Fife, where, apart from one or two small private lines, the N.B.R had a near monopoly. A final point is the expansionary activities of the N.B.R northwards, to include not only such lines as the Edinburgh

Perth and Dundee but, possibly much more ambitious schemes like an independent line to Aberdeen and, north from there into what later became Great North of Scotland Railway territory, arising from a petition from that city. There is no doubt about Richard Hodgson's ambitions to expand the company of which he was chairman. For example, when the Border Union line was opened on 1st.July 1862, a celebratory dinner was held at Carlisle. Hodgson in an after dinner speech, revealed the ambition to extend the N.B.R not just to Carlisle but to Inverness and the North. He said this in the presence of Kinloch, the chairman of the Highland Railway. Kinloch replied saying "I would be glad to hear at no distant day that the railway over which he presides was a possession of the N.B.R"(20). Having previously been prepared to consider a second main line between Edinburgh and Glasgow if the E & G.R fell into Caledonian hands, a move which proved unnecessary, Hodgson addressed employees of the E & G when his take-over had been accomplished, in the following terms; "eventually no doubt the Blane Valley and Milngavie branches will proceed by a line common to both to intersect the Oban & Callandar at or near Crianlarich" As Thomas put it "expansion was the Hodgson watchword" (21).

It will therefore come as no surprise that The Blyth & Tyne Railway now found itself the somewhat startled receiver of North British attention. The B&TR had been quietly putting its house in order during the period of the railway mania and thereafter without any spectacular involvement in railway speculation. As already mentioned the Morpeth branch was opened in 1858, being used by a considerable coal traffic from the Widdrington-Amble area to the Tyne staithes. This was followed in 1860 by the Dairy House to Tynemouth line, both these developments arising from the promotion of competing schemes. Finally on 28th June 1861 the Newcastle extension received parliamentary sanction. There seems little doubt that the N.B.R gave the B&T.R moral support, the latter being, as Tomlinson put it; "..not a little astonished at receiving so much flattering attention".(22)

A complication of the through route via the N.B.R, Border Counties, Wansbeck and Blyth & Tyne Railways was the peculiar track arrangement at Morpeth, diagramatically illustrated on page 37. Morpeth to Reedsmouth trains had to leave the B & T station heading in the wrong direction. They had to proceed eastwards to

The 1862 Agreement between the North British and
North Eastern Railways

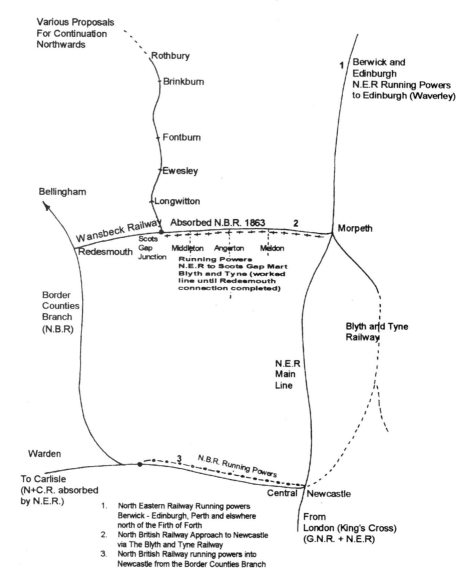

Various Proposals
For Continuation
Northwards

Rothbury

Brinkburn

Fontburn

Ewesley

Longwitton

Bellingham

Wansbeck Railway   Absorbed N.B.R. 1863   2

Scots
Gap   Middleton   Angerton   Meldon
Redesmouth   Junction
                         Running Powers
                         N.E.R to Scots Gap Mart
                         Blyth and Tyne (worked
                         line until Redesmouth
                         connection completed)

Morpeth

1   Berwick and
    Edinburgh
    N.E.R Running Powers
    to Edinburgh (Waverley)

Border
Counties
Branch
(N.B.R)

Blyth and Tyne
Railway

N.E.R
Main
Line

Warden

3   N.B.R. Running Powers

To Carlisle
(N+C.R. absorbed
by N.E.R.)

Central / Newcastle

From
London (King's Cross)
(G.N.R. + N.E.R)

1.   North Eastern Railway Running powers
     Berwick - Edinburgh, Perth and elswhere
     north of the Firth of Forth
2.   North British Railway Approach to Newcastle
     via The Blyth and Tyne Railway
3.   North British Railway running powers into
     Newcastle from the Border Counties Branch

Fontburn Viduct

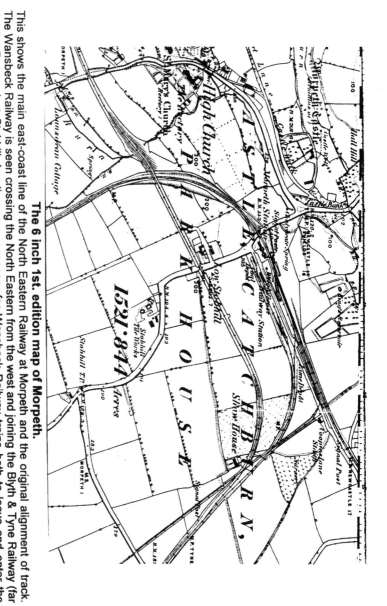

The 6 inch 1st. edition map of Morpeth.

This shows the main east-coast line of the North Eastern Railway at Morpeth and the original alignment of track. The Wansbeck Railway is seen crossing the North Eastern from the west and joining the Blyth & Tyne Railway (far right). Reversal at Stobhill Junction was necessary for Wansbeck Railway trains both to leave and enter the station, situated immediately to the south of the North Eastern Railway station. This cumbersome working practice was superseded at a later date when the connection spur west of Morpeth station was constructed. Stobhill was the home of Benjamin Woodman, solicitor to both the Wansbeck and Northumberland Central Railways.

36

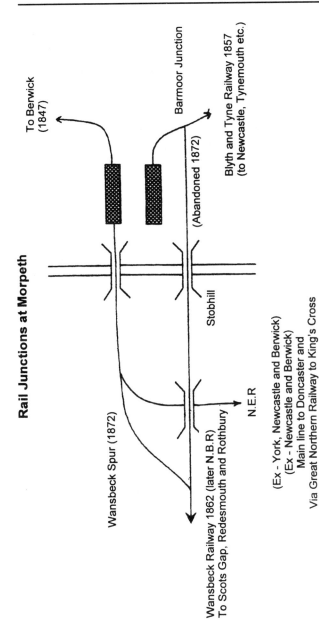

Rail Junctions at Morpeth

To Berwick
(1847)

Barmoor Junction

Blyth and Tyne Railway 1857
(to Newcastle, Tynemouth etc.)

(Abandoned 1872)

Wansbeck Spur (1872)

Stobhill

Wansbeck Railway 1862 (later N.B.R)
To Scots Gap, Redesmouth and Rothbury

N.E.R

(Ex - York, Newcastle and Berwick)
(Ex - Newcastle and Berwick)
Main line to Doncaster and
Via Great Northern Railway to King's Cross

The above is not to scale, and is diagramatic (see the 6 inch map for actual layout)
The essential features of note are the Stobhill Viaduct, Barmoor Junction and the Wansbeck
Spur and abandoned WR line of 1872.

Barmoor Junction, where reversal of direction took place. The trains then crossed the N.E.R main line by a bridge at Stobhill and so proceeded west. In an age of more leisurely journeying this procedure would not have raised an eyebrow as it does those of modern commentators, but there is little doubt that in the event of substantial through traffic from Edinburgh to Newcastle by this route, the N.B.R could have built a new station at Morpeth obviating this procedure. In any case, the opening up of this route to the N.B.R directors would have made no impact on through passenger traffic, but it would have enabled them to divert goods traffic away from the N.E.R. This would have been even more serious a threat if the bridge downstream from Newcastle had been built, with connections to rivals southwards such as The Hartlepool and Stockton & Darlington railways, as indicated earlier. In 1872 the N.E.R and N.B.R came to an agreement to build a joint line into Morpeth station (N.E.R.) This eased the problems imposed on the N.E.R which ran cattle traffic to and from Scots Gap mart. These trains required a North British employed pilotman. 1874 saw the swallowing up of the B & T R into the N.E.R which thus finally closed the door on any expansionary plans south-eastwards that the N.B.R might have continued to consider.

Chapter 4

Making a start

We have at last reached Northumberland Central territory in the form of Scots Gap station. The railway mania was by now long over, to be followed by the recession of 1858-9, a time when, as we have seen, the Border Counties and Wansbeck Railways were launched, struggled and eventually swallowed up by The North British. Further expansion of the Northumberland Railway network had to wait until 1862 when a new combination of promoters arose. These were some of the same landowners who had been involved in the Wansbeck scheme such as Earl Grey and Sir W.C. Trevelyan, but now they were joined by the formidable Richard Hodgson, no less, at the height of his power, being Chairman of the North British Railway and now an M.P. He had an interest in the Carham estate in North Northumberland. Railway historians often assume that he was a Northumberland landowner through this Carham estate connection, and he was the sort of man who might well have cared to give that impression. In fact this was not so, he merely marrying a co-heiress, becoming son-in-law of Lady Compton. The estate remained in the Compton family continuously from 1754 to 1919 when it passed from the family due to the last surviving heir being killed in The First World War(1). Nevertheless, Hodgson was now acting at least partly in his own right, whereas previously his association with the B.C.R and W.R had been purely as chairman of an investing company.

The proposed line was from Scots Gap to Rothbury, Thropton, Glanton, Wooler and Cornhill(2). This had already been considered earlier(3) by a meeting in Newcastle chaired by Trevelyan in which a much more ambitious Central Northumberland scheme from Newcastle to Kelso had been planned. This meeting issued a notice which was short and unambiguous in its resolutions reading as follows:

MEETING OF PROPRIETORS OF LAND AND OTHERS
INTERESTED IN HAVING A CENTRAL LINE OF
RAILWAY IN THE COUNTY OF NORTHUMBERLAND
6TH SEPTEMBER 1856
IN THE STATION HOTEL NEWCASTLE

Present: W.C Trevelyan; Ralph Carr Esq;
Waltar Selby Esq; John Grey Esq;
W.Snowball Esq; Thomas Gow Esq;
Joseph Snowball Esq; Rev Ogle.
W.C Trevelyan in the Chair

Resolved:
    1) That a line of railway proceeding from one of the existing trunk lines at or near Newcastle and passing through the County of Northumberland by Rothbury, Whittingham, Wooler, Beaumont and Cail[sic] Valleys to Scotland, uniting with the North British from Kelso to Melrose would be a great advantage. Goods; artificial manures and cattle food; produce to market; coal and lime.

    2) That from the population and character through which the line would pass, and in which it would terminate, there was every reason to believe that traffic would be remunerative.

    Why did the 1856 scheme fail to rouse interest whilst that of 1859 (admittedly at the end of the recession) prove more successful? The answer is not a simple one. In 1856, the ten year railway mania had virtually come to an end at a time of growing recession. Both public interest and available finance had waned. Secondly, the days of the amateur railway promoters were coming to an end. We now see the change from simple, sometimes naive amateurism, harnessed to the still rare but growing band of professionals, to more solid business practices with boards of well-heeled and level headed directors, making decisions on the advice of and information from career-structured senior officers, most of whom, allowing for some notable exceptions, were proficient. This led to many battles of the giants, ever ready to take advantage of predatory opportunities. In this case, the giants were The North Eastern and The North British Railways with the latter attempting expansion north and south, as already discussed.

    As much as he protested that he acted as an individual, it would be impossible for Richard Hodgson to completely divorce his interests. He must have known in 1862, when the N.C.R Bill was proposed that events were leading to the swallowing up of the Wansbeck, even if traffic along the full length of this line lay still in the future. He must have known of the key role Scots Gap junction would play. Indeed, it is documented that the N.C.R promoters actually expected the N.B.R or the N.E.R to work their services for them from the outset, on mutually satisfactory terms, a not uncommon practice(4). Thus, there is never any mention of locomotives or rolling stock in the early negotiations nor, at this stage in the capital investment of the N.C.R.

At the 1863 shareholders meeting, in proposing the adoption of a motion to proceed, Hodgson said *"The interest that he had in that railway [The N.C.R] was quite separate and apart from any railway interest that he might be supposed to have as being connected with the North British Company. He was not aware that the North British Co. was interested in the matter in the slightest degree with the exception of the benefit it might confer upon the Wansbeck Railway, in which the North British took a pecuniary interest. With respect to any other advantages supposed to be conferred on the North British Railway by the project, he could not perceive them; and he believed that the directors of the North British Company would deny altogether that they had any interest or concern in that undertaking. It was simply as a landowner [sic] connected with the district and as an inhabitant of the county [that] he should, for the sake of the community who were interested in it, use his best exertions to obtain the success or progress of that measure [The Bill], but on that account alone"*

Thus spoke the slippery-tongued entrepreneur and politician. Warn states that "...no sooner had the Wansbeck Railway scheme been piloted through Parliament than [in 1859] the N.B.R attempted to launch another major project called The Wooler Railway"(5) (map) This time the N.B.R was "frustrated". But collusion was in the air, with two rival camps involved. The one supported an Alnwick based branch serving Glendale with as one of several possibilities the leaving of a Rothbury line to other promoters. This would have suited the Alnwick faction, led by William Dickson, magistrates clerk, Chairman of the Alnwick Board of Health and a founder member of the Alnwick & County Bank. Dickson made his position clear, as follows:

"The people of Alnwick find that through the agency of the North British Railway Company, a survey is going on to make a line from their branch railway at or near Hawick, through the Vale of the Beaumont and by way of Wooler and Rothbury to the Wallington line

[sic] of railway near Cambo, by which they would probably push their traffic by means of lines already made, and to be made to Darlington [author's italics]. It is not impossible that by a little pressure The North British might make a branch to Alnwick, but the inhabitants have no wish to forward the views of that company with whose railway they are so closely connected by means of the present branch from Alnwick to Bilton."[Alnmouth station was originally named Bilton Junction]. In other words, Dickson was hedging his bets, using a stick-and-carrot approach to the N.E.R and had in mind the concept of the through Central Route by mentioning Darlington. Thus the Central Route concept was not confined to the North British, Midland and other big-league railway promoters but was understood at local level, a fact not always appreciated by commentators on the major companies.

The Alnwick Board of Health at its fortnightly meeting on Saturday February 22nd 1862 reported the prospects of a railway as follows:

"The question of railway accommodation was again brought forward; a meeting of proprietors and others connected with the Glendale Ward had to be held at Wooler on the 6th March to take into consideration the necessary steps for securing railway accommodation to that district. It was agreed to send a deputation from Alnwick to attend that meeting, to learn what measures were being adopted, and ascertain the probability of Alnwick being able to co-operate, or of being likely to be benefited by the course pursued at Wooler. The deputation from The Board appointed to attend at Wooler were Mr W.Dickson Senior, Mr Luke Hindmarsh and Mr John Thompson"

A special meeting of the Alnwick Board of Health was held on Friday August 15th 1862 to consider the proposed Glendale Railway, W.Dickson being in the chair. It was announced that a communication had been received from the directors of the North Eastern Railway appointing Friday 29th inst. as the day when they would meet the different committees of the district at Newcastle to confer as to the proposed line of rail from Alnwick to Cornhill. The attendance of the Glendale, Wooler and Cornhill districts had been secured.

The 1859 proposal was immediately challenged by one of

the following year. This emanated from the other Alnwick based group, supported by the Alnwick Mercury. A line was surveyed by Thomas Thompson of Alnwick, consisting of a twenty two mile route to Wooler, following roughly the line ultimately built by the N.E.R, but with some important differences, together with various options for branches. The map deposited with the Northumberland Record Office shows the line leaving Alnwick, where a junction was made with the Alnwick-Bilton Junction line, and thence curving south west via Rugley and St Margarets to Glen Aln. From here a further loop ran via Overthwaits and Hillhead, to the West of Broome Park and so to cross the Aln at Whittingham. This would increase the journey time by extra mileage and sharper curves, but reduce the construction costs substantially, as compared with the 1881 North-Eastern Alnwick-Coldstream line because the expensive works over Alnwick Moor and through Hillhead Tunnel of the latter were eliminated. Between Whittingham and Wooler the only significant deviation was at Lilburn where the line, instead of passing through Ilderton station veered east to pass between Lilburn Tower and Lilburn Grange. The line to Wooler is outlined in red. From there, northwards, a blue "extension" passed via Akeld, Kirknewton and Yetholm (Cherryburn), and thence between Greenlees and Blacklaw to Wooden and Kelso. The plan is signed Thomas Thompson, Surveyor, Alnwick and dated 1861.

It has been said that the Alnwick proposals were not serious attempts to have a line constructed, being merely blocking tactics, but the detail in this survey must run contrary to that view. The prospectus of this proposed line is for a railway from Alnwick to Wooler of 22 miles length, the preamble including the Beaumont Valley, Yetholm and Kelso. It was to be of single line construction with land purchased for doubling. It included a viaduct over the Lemmington Burn to the Bridge of Aln and the cost was estimated at £143,000 or £6,500 per mile. Estimates of traffic potential were: coal 13,400 tons, utilising Shilbottle and Newton on the Moor coalfields and later, Alnwick, Denwick etc. Lime was estimated at 158,360 tons. Limestone would be from Shilbottle, Whittle and Newton on the Moor, Alnwick Moor and Hibberlaw; there was also said to be "superior freestone, ironstone, basalt and fire clay". The income from freight traffic etc. was based on Alnwick - Wooler but "the railway will be made to Wooler and carried forward to other places as necessary" His Grace the Duke of Northumberland was said to be favourably disposed towards the scheme (in a letter from Hugh Taylor, secretary to the Committee of the Local Board of Health of Alnwick, dated at Alnwick Castle on the 9th March 1861. This is of some importance when we consider the attitude of The Dukes to the financial difficulties of the N.C.R at a later date) The view of the North Eastern directors is contained in a letter from the Secretary of the N.E.R which says merely that Mr Harrison "is to make a general survey of the district"[on behalf of that company](6). T.E Harrison was a civil engineer and surveyor of wide experience, employed on an occasional basis by the N.E.R for independent judgements. It seems hard to justify the view that this was a mere blocking tactic against the rival Alnwick scheme when the matter was gone into in such great detail.

Rather, these Alnwick proposals were based on hard economic facts of life. The traders saw their livelihood derived from the Alnwick hinterland reduced. Many still felt the ties with the N.E.R should be strengthened, even allowing for the fact that there was still resentment at the bypassing of Alnwick by the Newcastle & Berwick main line. This was felt to be inexcusable, despite the provision of a branch from Bilton,(7). In the end, the pro-N.E.R faction won so that the Thompson-surveyed line was very similar to that adopted for the Alnwick-Cornhill railway of 1882. Nevertheless, the N.E.R Board, which always took a cautious view of branch-line proposals, did not show great interest, even after, or perhaps because of Harrison's report. His views differed from Thompson's in suggesting a route through Hulne Park, and also included an extension north to Edinburgh. This would have been much cheaper and easier to work, but was clearly not to find any favour with The Duke of Northumberland. This route certainly can be regarded as a mere exercise in 'blocking', or perhaps rather shrewd public relations, as it would throw the onus of failure onto the shoulders of others including The Duke and those promoters unable to find funding for the extension to Edinburgh.(8)

The reason for the successful N.C.R promotion of 1862, lay largely in the fact that the Border Counties and Wansbeck Railways were by now in the process of being incorporated into the N.B.R. The N.C.R had strong support from an impressive list of landed gentry, whose interest lay in improving transport to their estates. The Hodgson-led expansionary N.B.R can be seen at work behind the scenes. Moore(9) cites the case of the proposed line, already mentioned, from Morpeth to St Boswells of 1854. Although plans were never deposited, the survey of this line was made by Locke and Errington, indicates that the 1854 intentions were real enough. If so, it is likely that the North British was connected because, significantly, St Boswells was the proposed junction, then on the route of the N.B.R central thrust southwards. The easier N.E.R route to, say, Cornhill was ignored, notwithstanding a further petition from the inhabitants of Coldstream to the directors of the N.E.R. The conclusions are obvious.

Whilst one Alnwick lobby would have preferred a direct line to Kelso because of the trade and other contacts between these towns, the N.B.R preferred route was to Cornhill as being nearer to Berwick and, indeed, nearer to the Richard Hodgson power-base at Carham. One possible Central Route, of which there is no record of consideration, even by later railway authors but which surely must have been in the minds of the North British Directors, would have utilised the N.B.R main line from Berwick to Edinburgh, not normally traffic-saturated and then via the Northumberland Central territory to reach the south. This would have had the advantage of being a cheap option, for example, far less costly than the Border Union route. Indirect evidence for this lies in the opening paragraphs of the Northumberland Central Railway Act which describes the northern end of the line as being *in the parish of Ford with a Cornhill branch* [(author's italics)] Success in 1863 lay in the backing of a powerful N.B.R lobby at Westminster. The run up to the presentation involved J.F Tone, whom we met earlier on the Border Counties, and who would ultimately be retained to survey the line. He made his position clear with comments at a Morpeth promotional meeting as far back as 1859. These make interesting reading:

"The object of the line was to intersect, in a north and south direction, the central portion of the county; and the construction of the Wansbeck line having been authorised, rendered it more easy than it would otherwise have been". Tone was a man thinking in terms of the long central route(10).

The Bill followed meetings begun in 1859 and lasting to 1862. These involved all parties. The Alnwick Committee held them in such places as Wooler. Sir Horace St Paul of Ewart was a leading supporter and is quoted in the press as stating the promoters should "impress on the North Eastern the strong feelings of landowners and farmers.....in favour of this line"(11). This is of significance because later he changed allegiance, becoming a director of the N.C.R., thus indicating that his interests lay in obtaining a railway connection for Glendale and that he did not appear to favour one major company more than the other. At this stage others were prepared to hedge their bets e.g. Ralph Carr of Hedgeley is reported as stating that *"whilst he thought it their duty ......to conciliate the good will of the great North Eastern...neither Alnwick nor Wooler should consider themselves at the mercy of one railway"*(12). The pro-North Eastern Alnwick faction was able to muster 250 signatures to a petition to the N.E.R (still with no effect). The fact that it lost the battle did not mean that it lost the war, as will appear eventually.

Rival meetings were held in places such as Coldstream, Crookham, Wooperton and Glanton as well as the only two towns of any size on the projected N.C.R line, Rothbury and Wooler. Committees were formed which took their responsibilities seriously. For example, one committee meeting at Glanton on 1st March 1864 was specifically demanding that the directors of the Northumberland Central Railway build a station at Glanton i.e. not a station serving several local villages including Whittingham, Hedgley etc. This was of course not to be, because the ultimate financial troubles meant that the line was never built beyond Rothbury. The final decisions with regard to the route proposed rested not just with J.F Tone, the professional engineer concerned, but with enthusiasm and more importantly financial backing for the line and, in one case a memorial to the Bill from the Cornhill estate, whose trustees objected on the grounds that the estate would be "injuriously intersected" by the junction with the Coldstream branch(13). Thus the extension to Coldstream was abandoned as a result of general lack of interest in that town, lack of funds from that quarter, and the above mentioned memorial of objection, as reported by Woodman, now N.C.R secretary. On the other hand, Sir Horace St Paul's enthusiasm, appearing in eloquent rhetoric was backed with the promise of hard cash. He was following in the footsteps of his father as a noteworthy estate improver at Ewart Park. He was a supporter of the Lands Improvement Co, a kind of credit union or as Sewell describes it "a sort of Victorian Hire Purchase Co" (14). The Terminal Annuity figures provided by Sir Horace gave the estimate for his estate by this company as £40,000. He stated that he was prepared to contribute a further £70,000. His professional advisers were of the opinion that his estate would be improved by this method to the extent of £3000 p.a.(15). The agent to The Lands Improvement Co, John Dickson of Saughton, estimated that because of its involvement with the railway 54,000 acres of arable land and an unspecified area of grazing land would be improved, the latter by 6d per acre. The novelty of this method of funding aroused much interest. The Railway Times of 14th February 1863, quoted by Jenkins(16), gives credit for the successful negotiations of this to Richard Hodgson and enthuses over the way in which landowners retain all rights over their own property whilst the land is improved, an early example of the coexistence of private inheritance and public benefit. Clearly one must regard all the above figures, particularly those quoted by Horace St Paul as being at the least, suspect. The fatal flaw in the scheme, however, was that the railway had to be completed and opened to the public throughout before The Enclosure Commissioners could grant loans, but "shares in the capital of the company subscribed for, or held by such a landowner, or so many of such shares as are equal in nominal amount to the money advanced by The Lands Improvement Company, and authorised to be charged, must be fully paid up in cash". We shall see in a later chapter how matters did not work out.

The above meeting took place at Morpeth in February 1863. This followed logically the meeting of 27th October 1862 in the Morpeth office of the Central Northumberland Railway. Earl Grey was in the chair and the executive committee included Richard Hodgson, George Grey, Sir W.T Trevelyan Bart, William Lowrey, T. Mason, Waltar Johnson , J Orde, Waltar Selby, and the Chairmen and Vice-chairmen of the following local committees still to be formed: Coldstream (but see above) Wooler, Aln Valley and Coquet Valley when £2000 was indicated as the cost of promotion of the Bill. This was thought to present little difficulty for emotions were running high as it coincided with the first section of the Wansbeck Railway being completed. Sir Walter Trevelyan indicated that he did not wish to continue to act as chairman because he already acted in this capacity for the Wansbeck Railway to which he was heavily committed.(When The Bill was being promoted and immediately after the Act was obtained, the Chairman was Earl Grey.) Benjamin Woodman issued a notice indicating the constitution of the Executive Committee and expanded on the raising of funds as follows:

"The capital was to be raised initially by shares not loans. There would be powers for landowners to take up shares on the proposed line to the extent of the increased value that construction of the line will apply to their estates shares so taken up will be deposited with the Inclosure Commissioners, and shall belong to the estate so charged; and further no rent charge upon their estate for the above purpose shall be larger than the Inclosure Commissioners approve, having reference to the increased value of the land from the construction of the line".

Because of the novelty of funding at the time by this method, The Lands Improvement Co aroused great interest in railway circles. A summary of the situation as it developed with regard to The Northumberland Central Railway is therefore appropriate.

As indicated earlier, the N.C.R was not able to raise the 10% deposit required by Act of Parliament, within the time limit stipulated. This sum was £20,800 and the law required it to be deposited with the Court of Chancery. The company therefore borrowed from The Lands Improvement Co to reach the required figure. However the Lands Improvement Co had no powers, even under the amendment of 1859 to fund schemes prior to completion, when loans etc could be expected to be repaid.

Lands Improvement Co money was intended for items of infrastructure such as drainage, fencing, road access improvement etc. The Amending Act of 1859 empowered it to lend money to individual estates on a 25 year rental, in anticipation of improved value of that estate, either at sale value, in terms of raised rentals, or improved income from better returns on demesne land etc.

In this case, Messrs Warings, the contractors, agreed to meet the Lands Improvement Co liability up to a maximum figure, which was written into their contract with The N.C.R. It was not unusual for construction companies to take shares as part of their contract, these being of no benefit until the work was finished and dividends were beginning to be declared. This investment was an extension of that procedure, but clearly differed in that benefits to the constructing company could not be anticipated in the manner of dividends.

At the February 1863 meeting, the N.C.R decided to raise

CENTRAL NORTHUMBERLAND RAILWAY COMPANY, LIMITED.

STATEMENT OF AFFAIRS.

RECEIPTS	£	s.	d.
Amount Due or Paid on Calls :—			
Sir Charles Edward Trevelyan, Bart, K.C.B.	1,000	0	0
Ralph Carr Ellison, Esq.	2,000	0	0
Hon. F. W. Lambton. M.P.	500	0	0
Sir John Swinburne, Bart.	500	0	0
Sir Arthur E. Middleton, Bart.	500	0	0
Walter Charles Selby, Esq.	1,000	0	0
Percival Fenwick Clennell, Esq.	250	0	0
Rev. J. E. Elliot-Bates	200	0	0
Henry Bell, Esq.	100	0	0
Rev. W. Pitt Trevelyan	100	0	0
Ernest Augustus Percival, Esq.	100	0	0
John Robinson, Esq.	250	0	0
Henry T. Morton, Esq.	100	0	0
J. D. Wealleans, Esq.	100	0	0
G. P. Hughes, Esq.	100	0	0
B. P. Selby, Esq.	10	0	0
Albert Grey, Esq., M.P.	10	0	0
Henry Willoughby Trevelyan, Esq.	50	0	0
W. E. Beck, Esq.	50	0	0
William Murray, Esq., M.D.	50	0	0
Miss Florence T. Trevelyan	50	0	0
William Forster, Jun., Esq.	30	0	0
George A. Grey, Esq.	20	0	0
Thomas Leighton, Esq.	20	0	0
Rev. George Hans Hamilton	10	0	0
A. M. Dunn, Esq.	200	0	0
Wm. Orde, Esq.	30	0	0
Roddam John Roddam, Esq.	100	0	0
E. Carr, Esq.	10	0	0
Edward Keeles, Esq.	20	0	0
Edward Ridley, Esq.	10	0	0
Andrew Montagu, Esq.	1,000	0	0
H. Milvain, Esq.	208	0	0
James Smith, Esq.	20	0	0
	£8,698	**0**	**0**

PAYMENTS.	£	s.	d.
Cheque Book	0	10	0
1 William Shelford, C.E.	1,000	0	0
2 R. B. Reid, Newcastle Chronicle	18	3	0
3 John Ritchie and Co., Scotsman	34	8	7
4 Geo. Armstrong & Sons, and C. D. Forster	600	0	0
5 Lambton and Company	8	11	4
6 John Smith, Kelso Mail	27	13	0
7 Geo. Armstrong & Sons, and C. D. Forster	22	5	0
8 Spottiswood and Company	10	10	6
9 Lambert and Company	4	14	6
10 Lambert and Company	13	13	0
11 R. Redpath, Newcastle Journal	6	10	6
12 George Cunningham, C.E.	136	10	0
13 T. G. Bewick, C.E.	131	13	3
14 G. A. Labour	26	7	2
15 Moses Pye	43	14	6
16 Ralph Hedley	17	15	0
17 John Clay	32	19	0
18 William Moses	5	5	0
19 Dr. Richardson	12	0	0
20 William Rochester	13	9	0
21 A. Calder	19	10	8
22 Ephraim Arkle	15	0	0
23 William Thompson	22	6	10
24 H. H. Scott	13	1	0
25 J. Angus	6	18	7
26 J. Bonnor	27	11	6
27 C. McC. Swarbreck	73	10	0
28 Lambton & Co., (Interest on Deposit, &c.)	1,032	6	1
29 Messrs. Leadbitter and Harvey	19	17	3
30 John Jordan	31	10	0
31 C. D. Forster	67	3	1
32 D. F. Wilson	2	0	0
33 William Shelford, C.E.	1,501	1	8
34 J. C. Rees	963	4	1
35 J. C. Rees	95	12	0
36 Mr. Pope, Q.C.	261	9	0
37 Mr. Milvain	298	7	0
38 Mr. Balfour Brown	208	7	6
39 Mr. Faber	189	10	6
40 C. D. Forster (Salary, and disbursements as Secretary)	28	3	0
41 Geo. Armstrong & Sons, and C. D. Forster's Charges and Disbursements, viz. :— £1,721 1s. 0d., less £600, and £22 5s. 0d., and the £22 5s. 0d., got back when first set of Notes were cancelled, in all— £644 10s. 0d.	1,076	11	0
42 Mr. John Robinson (Checking Traffic)	2	10	0
Balance	590	4	5
	£8,698	**0**	**0**

SUMMARY OF STATEMENT.

	£	s.	d.
Amount Paid or due on Calls	3,098	0	0
	£3,698	**0**	**0**

	£	s.	d.	£	s.	d.
ENGINEERING.—Survey and Plans for Deposit	1,855	0	0			
Estimate, and before Committee	649	1	3			
				2,504	1	3
WITNESSES.						
Before Committee				600	3	6
				Brought forward	3,104	5	2
LAW EXPENSES :—						
Counsels' Fees before Committee	907	14	6			
Parliamentary Agents' Charges and Disbursements	1,058	16	1			
Do. Mr. Jordan	31	10	0			
Solicitors' Charges and Disbursements, less £22 5s. 0d., Stamps Returned, and £250 allowed off Bill of Costs	1,698	16	0			
				3,696	16	7
SUNDRIES :—						
Interest on Deposits and Stamps	1,040	17	5			
Printing and Advertising	148	3	1			
Preliminary Expenses	87	0	4			
Checking Traffic	2	10	0			
Secretary's Salary and Payments	28	8	0			
				1,306	13	10
Balance				590	4	5
				£3,698	**0**	**0**

Examined and found correct.

JOHN ROBINSON.

capital in this way. Land owners could apply if their estates were on or near, and therefore likely to benefit from the line of railway. They could take shares in the company in the form of rents, proportionate to the anticipated value of the land. These rents were only chargeable to tenants after the line was running and benefits being received. The only condition placed upon the landowner was that the Lands Improvement Co had to have financial guarantees. Earl Grey tried to have the matter of the application for loans clarified because doubts were expressed as to the legal availability of such funds. He, as Chairman, moved in The House of Lords that a select committee be appointed to enquire into the availability of cash to the N.C.R in this way. Lord Redesdale, Chairman of Select Committees, ruled that such a measure would need to be presented separately, as it would create a legal precedent for all railways. An Act was promoted in 1864, and became law as The Improvement of Lands Act. This covered all aspects of loans without specific reference to the N.C.R

The financial arrangements were not still suitable for situations in which the N.C.R found itself. Funds still had to come in from new shares and calls on shareholders. These were coming in only slowly so that the 10% deposit was not yet obtainable. Capital had to be reasonably 'in-the-pipeline' for secure loans to be made. Neither land owners nor tenants were happy with the 'jam-tomorrow' situation, particularly landowners who were entailed, and those with private doubts about the whole scheme such as The Duke of Northumberland and Lord Ravensworth. Others, like Sir Horace St Paul were committed enthusiasts, and clearly had vastly unrealistic expectations of the new financing procedures. Tenants were often not co-operative. This arose for a variety of reasons, such as short term leases, tenants plans to move elsewhere before the benefits of cheaper coal, lime, livestock movement worked through to them, having become effective over a period of build-up. Landlords had to be fully committed to the railway and its financing. If not, many tenants would feel insecurity in the situation and be reluctant to agree to pay increased rents. The N.C.R tried to get round this problem by drawing up a form of agreement between landlord and tenant, in which an attempt was made to protect the interests of both parties. It was not received with wild enthusiasm.

The position reflected in the crisis of July 1864, when differences arose in interpretation of the financial situation between

Messrs Waring and The Board. The latter stated that the £50,000 goal required by law and by the contract to allow work to start had been attained. The former pointed out that this was only reached with the aid of Lands Improvement Co funding and were less than convinced of the case. The result was litigation(17).

Moore argues the case that the promoters and directors were Whigs, implying political motivation to their interest. This may well be true, but, it could be chance which ordained an essentially estate railway, "in a strongly Whig county", passing through Whig estates and happening to avoid ones owned by the more ardent Tories. Indeed, Moore immediately proceeds to state one powerful motive for Trevelyan's interest, far removed from politics. His land had very good quality limestone producing top-quality lime. This could not be matched by lime produced in the north of the county either in quality or price. George Grey at Milfield and George Culley at Fowberry were, through their revolutionary methods of agriculture, firm friends and in need of good transport. Earl Grey and Sir John Swinburne were just "railway men" to the marrow, as indicated in references to them elsewhere. There were several Tories on the list, but only Earl Grey was in the highest political league. A more telling overview is that of lack of expertise in railway and related business practice. Thus, we find W.Forster of Burradon writing to George Grey in 1864 advising him of the meeting of the N.C.R at the Queen's Head, Morpeth, asking "if you are elected a director, will you accept? We are much in need of men of business in the directorship and I know none more competent than yourself.....Can you contract me with your proxy?" George Grey in a much later but undated letter writes to G. Dunn; "As we have now so nearly obtained the sum required to enable us to complete the Cambo and Rothbury section of the Central Railway and that much by the aid of several gentlemen who can have no interest in the line as a convenience, I trust that gentlemen like yourself who must be much advantaged by the line, will not allow it to be given up, as must shortly be the case if we do not get a little timely support. I venture to hope that you will not leave us without your share of assistance"(18). These letters to and from Grey neatly summarise the events that were about to unfold.

A minor point of interest shows the Trevelyan influence in a very down-to-earth way. The hotel built at Scots Gap (now the headquarters of the National Trust in Northumbria) to meet the needs of travellers on both the Wansbeck and Northumberland Central Railways was a Temperance Hotel; you had to go for a long walk in order to get an alcoholic beverage in you lived in Trevelyan country! This was not a new feature of the district with the arrival of the railway. In coaching days, a letter of October 1847 written to the press complains that *"....at the Queen's Head, Cambo, I ordered dinner and was surprised that no ale, spirits or wine was available.....the license taken from the house, but there was no complaint or disturbance, just the magistrates pleasing Sir Waltar Trevelyan......"* Years later The Temperance Trevelyans hadn't changed their views. Preserved in the archives is correspondence between Trevelyan and the aged George Stephenson with regard to the sale of intoxicating liquor at railway stations. The question asked was "Did Stephenson find any problem with it on The Stockton and Darlington?" The answer, basically may not have been one that Trevelyan expected, it being summed up as "not with the passengers, but certainly with the train crews!" (19).

A meeting of shareholders in the summer of 1863 was told that land had been staked out and purchases of land and settlement of rentals claims were progressing. Terms for the Southern Terminus to Rothbury were agreed and several miles at the northern end. The Scots Gap to Rothbury section alone was to be proceeded with at present. The Bill was prepared. Capital on the first call was a sum of £4,921 9s 0d and interest £794 12s 2d. This enabled the directors to liquidate all the engagements of the company to 31st January 1864.

The Bill, with Parliamentary Agents Messrs Pritt & Co to promote it, and alledgedly backed by a powerful North British lobby in Parliament required a deposit of 8% on the £260,000 capital called for to be placed with the Accountant General. This presented an immediate financial problem because only £23,810 had been promised by the date of the February meeting. The deposit to be made came to £20,800 and £2000 (estimated) was required to present The Bill. At the February 1863 meeting Mr Benjamin Woodman, was appointed secretary and read out a list of expenses so far, which included such items as printing, advertising, surveying, drawing up plans etc as coming to £1,892. That meant that the coffers were empty, and reliance was being made on £9,400 which The Secretary stated would be the sum accruing from The Lands

NORTHUMBERLAND CENTRAL RAILWAY

Suggestions to Owners and Occupiers of Land on and continuous to the above Line of Railway as to raising capital

When money is borrowed under the Lands Improvement'Act, for Draining, Railways, or other improvements, an annual Rent Charge is imposed upon the land, which pays the Interest on the amount raised, and in 25 years clears off the debt. The half-yearly payments are the same during the whole term, but each half-year a larger proportion of the sum paid goes towards diminishing the debt, and a smaller amount is required for Interest. Thus if £1,000 is borrowed, and the Interest of Money is £4 10s. 0d. per cent, (which is probably about the present rate,) the annual Rent Charge imposed upon the Estate would be £67 (or £6 14s. per cent.), and each half -yearly payment would be £33 10s. Of the first half-yearly payment, £10 17s. 2d. would be repayment of Capital, and £22 17s. 3d. would be for Interest; in the last half-year of the Term, only between 15 and 16 shillings would be payable for Interest, and the rest would go to paying off the last part of the debt. When a Loan is got from the Lands Improvement Company, the Rent Charge deed contains a table which shows how much of each half-yearly payment is for Interest, and how much for repayment of Capital, so that at the end of any number of years by looking at this table it can be seen at once how much of the debt still remains due, and how much has been paid off.

The Act of Parliament which enables Land owners to borrow Money on their Estates for Railways provide that the Shares bought with the Money so raised shall be deposited with the Enclosure Commissioners until the debt is paid off; but the Act also provides, that in proportion as it is paid, the Landowner may re-lease a corresponding number of Shares, of which he then becomes the absolute owner.

These provisions of the Act put it into the power of the Tenants of Farms on the Line of the projected Central Railway, to do much towards supplying the Capital required for the early completion of the Line without any loss to themselves. Though the Landowners on the Line have shown a strange indifference to the success of the scheme, it is not probable that many of them would refuse to raise money on their Estates to take Shares in the Railway, if the Tenants on their part would offer to pay the Rent Charges on their Farms during the term of their occupations, on condition of their receiving as many Shares as they might thus pay for. It is believed that few Farms on the Line would be able to save less than one pair of Horses by the opening of the Railway, and that £100 a year would therefore be a moderate calculation of what the Framer would gain by it. Some would gain much more, some no doubt less, be each Farmer would easily calculate what Rent Charges he could afford to pay for the advantages of having the Railway made.

It is suggested that if the Tenants on the Line would combine together and make in writing a proposal to their Landlords for an arrangement of this kind, the whole of the Capital required for the speedy completion of the Railway might be raised at once. It is obvious that whether Tenants hold their Farms for year to year or on lease, and if on lease for how long a term, would make no difference as to coming to an arrangement of this kind. The bargain would simply be that from the time of the opening of the Railway the Tenants would pay a Rent Charge proportioned to the advantage he derived from it, and that according to the greater or smaller number of years during which he continued to hold his Farm, he would become entitled to more or fewer Shares.

The form of an undertaking which it is proposed that the Tenants would be asked to sign is added.

53

Improvement Co. Nevertheless, enthusiasm was not dampened and Sir George Grey, Sir M.W Ridley (another of the converts to the N.C.R) and Richard Hodgson agreed to present The Bill. The Secretary, civil engineer and auditors agreed to take only working expenses until such time as there was income. This situation was a far cry from the expectations voiced at the previous meeting, just four months back, when a return on capital of "at least 5%" was promised and the request was made for a deposit of 25/- per £10 shares. A question that was to cause problems later was put to J.F.Tone in the presence of the auditor, namely how did the anticipated costs of construction compare with the Wansbeck Railway per mile? J.F.Tone thought that they would be a little more than that of the W.R which had been "rather less than £5000 per mile". This could be, and perhaps was later, misconstrued.

Some people, however, were less than enthusiastic, or at least tempered their euphoria with sound business sense. Such an attitude could be expected from that shrewd entrepreneurial farmer, George Grey who presented the N.C.R with "A Memorandum of My Final Withdrawal" dated June 1st 1863. In a lengthy document he said:

"....I demurred to signing [his share application] because there was only a little more than 320,000 of shares taken and I feared that the county would not come forward in taking shares which would leave the directors and company in a dilemma with contractors who, finding themselves unsupported by shares would withdraw from the undertaking, leaving the company (i.e. Lord Grey, myself and perhaps, Sir W Trevelyan) to bear the chief loss and liabilities. I said that I thought such an undertaking as this for the county agricultural interests ought to be carried out in a very different manner - not by a few gentlemen showing it through without money and without friends - but by a nobility and gentry of the county with a large majority and ample resources. Mr Hodgson and Mr Woodman represented that my withdrawal might be fatal to the·undertaking". He then stated how he had withdrawn to seek legal advice and after some difficulty, a Mr Hickley had read over his copy of the agreement and accompanied him to meet Mr Hodgson and one of the firm of Pritt & Co, when after debate he formally withdrew from the undertaking and directed Messrs Pritt to strike his name out from the list of directors in the Bill. He later said *"that if two thirds of the shares were taken*

*up I might take £3000 in shares and accept shares for my land ....
and give my support in a private capacity".* Hodgson and Woodman
reproved him as "the originator and promoter of the scheme". I said
*"this was a great mistake. I was not the originator. I first joined it by
attending a public meeting at Wooler where some expected I would
oppose it."* Earl Greys letter of reply merely stated that he saw no
problems with the scheme(20). Thus the Board lost a man who would
have been its most capable director.

The Bill for the promotion of the Northumberland Central
Railway was duly presented and The Act received the royal assent
on 28th July 1863.,(26 & 27 Vic. cap 335) within a few days of the
Act allowing the North British to absorb the Wansbeck Railway. As
expected the capital was £260,000 in £10 shares, the estimate being
£250,000 from Scots Gap to the Berwick & Kelso at Cornhill with an
additional £10,000 in event of an extension to Coldstream. The Act
was somewhat loose in its definitions stating quite rightly that the
line commenced in the parish of Hartburn, by a junction with the
Wansbeck Railway, and terminating in the parish of Ford, in the same
county. *This was the main-line to which, rather oddly, was added a
railway "(hereinafter called the Cornhill Station Branch) from the main
line at Ford terminus thereof, to the Berwick and Kelso branch of the
North Eastern Railway in the parish of Norham."* The route was to
include Alwinton and Norham, both specifically mentioned. There
may have been ulterior motives behind this wording, because, as
indicated earlier, there were at least rumours of railway developments
immediately across The Border. In fact, the Kelso Chronicle of 4th
March 1864 reported on the Beaumont branch of the Kelso,
Morebattle and Yetholm Railway." *The idea of a railway along the
valleys of the Kale, Beaumont and Glen had long been familiar to
the public and was advocated in our columns many years ago... The
construction of the Central Northumberland Railway [sic] will remove
what was always a difficulty in the way, by opening up an outlet to
traffic at the farthest end of the line. It is now proposed that the line
leave the Jedburgh branch of the N.B.R at Ormiston station, then
proceed by Eckford, Blinkbonny and Marlefield to Morebattle. Then
it would go by way of Linton Burnfoot and Primside along the south
side of Yetholm Loch, and past Lochtower to Town Yetholm from
which it will be carried by Bowmont Hill, Mindrum and Howtle to join
the C.N.R at Millfied ...there would be little expense and the support*

of the N.B.R directors was expected". Needless to say, nothing came of this scheme, but at the time, it clearly influenced thinking south of The Border where the Thompson, Alnwick Route, was trying to tempt it to build to Wooler, whilst the Directors of the N.C.R merely kept their options open.(21).

The usual safeguards were inserted to prevent adverse practices affecting the Wansbeck branch of the N.B.R (as it now was) at Scots Gap and similarly The Kelso branch of the N.E.R at Cornhill, with powers of arbitration by The Board of Trade. The Act stipulated that The Wansbeck Railway could employ staff, erect signals etc at their own discretion to manage the new junction arrangements and the N.C.R would have to meet the costs. However the N.C.R was empowered to make agreements with the "Wansbeck Railway, North Eastern Railway Co and The North British Railway Co , or any one or more of them, relating to working, maintenance, traffic interchange, tolls and charges etc." Furthermore joint committees were allowed. This wording of the Act is worthy of consideration in its stringent safeguards for existing railways on the one hand and opportunities for co-operation on the other. It seems as if no objections were raised at Committee stage, and we can assume tolerance if not active collusion in framing this section of The Act. We have already noted how there was expectation of further promotions in the wording of the Border Counties Bill. Here we are near to an implied assumption of expansion and take-over by one of the larger companies, even The Blyth and Tyne was not ruled out.

The report of the Executive Committee to subscribers, Earl Grey being the Chairman, announcing the passage of The Act was circulated in August 1863. It read:

"The Bill is through parliament with the petitions against it being from The Trustees of Mr Collingwood's estate at Cornhill resulting in the abandonment to Coldstream (there being, as we know, a failure of guarantees of those who particularly advocated this extension.) A petition by the North Eastern Railway had been concerned with the junction at Cornhill, but this was now satisfactorily agreed. A minor petition by Mr Burdon of Wooperton as to how the line progressed through his land had also been dealt with. The total fees were £5,654 19s 1d

It is understood that so soon as a sufficient amount of local subscription had been obtained, the whole line will be simultaneously constructed, and the easy nature of the works will permit of its being opened for public traffic within eighteen months after the contractors shall be in possession of the land". This was repeated on 1st October, again signed by Earl Grey as Chairman

How wrong could one be?. Yet the optimistic tone had some justification. The Jedburgh Railway had been completed at under £5000 per mile, whilst the Cockermouth, Keswick and Penrith Railway, a line of about equal length and promoted about the same time, was promoted, the capital raised and construction completed in two years. The difference was that these lines each served a specific purpose without undue competition with others, which was plain for all to see. Thus The Jedburgh Railway served one town on a short branch from the N.B.R and was easily and quickly absorbed into the latter. The Cockermouth, Keswick and Penrith was required by two parties, iron ore and coking coal traffic between Durham and the Cumbrian Coast and the opening up of The Lake District for the new rich industrialists of Lancashire and Yorkshire. The Northumberland Central Railway, whilst having objectives for individual landowners and traders, had no such clear-cut general objectives.

Chapter 5

Slow progress

The last chapter ended when royal assent was given to the Northumberland Central Railway Bill on 28th July 1863. This may suggest that the hard work was over but, in fact, the railway's troubles were only just beginning. The Newcastle Daily Journal of February 21st 1864 noted the Wansbeck Railway half yearly meeting on the previous day held at the Queen's Head, Morpeth. Richard Hodgson was heavily involved here as he would be on the very next day in the same venue when his concern would be the half-yearly meeting of the N.C.R. The choice of meeting place may well have been for the sake of convenience but, what is surprising is that no mention is made of either at the other's meeting. This is remarkable, as the two lines were to be connected at Scots Gap Junction. They would to some degree depend upon the other, and because a number of the same people were involved. Ulterior motives may have been at work, for example, Richard Hodgson may have deliberately wished to play down his major involvement in the two schemes. If so, this can only be a part of his railway politics emanating from the N.B.R.

The N.C.R meeting the next day became a minor piece of local railway folk-lore. Sir John Swinburne was in the chair but no shareholders were present and not even a quorum of directors. The formal meeting was postponed for six months, there being no other choice. However, at the request of Hodgson it was agreed that an informal debate should take place amongst those present. He argued that it was still right for the public and shareholders to know the position of the company. He then stated that since the last half yearly meeting, the line had been staked out, and negotiations for the purchase of land had progressed, as had the settlement of tenants' claims for interference with their occupations. He complained about the failure of subscribers to come forward, following this by a description of the Terminable Annuities Act which was imminent. The directors earnestly requested co-operation of the shareholders in this and other matters. Receipts on account of the first call on 3,157 shares amounted to the sum of £4,921 9s 0d. This enabled the directors to liquidate expenses up to 31st January 1864. The cash in hand was £662 4s 0d. He proposed that a further call of £2 per share should be made and this was seconded by Mr Bolam. That this was contrary to established practice in the absence of a quorum seems certain, as must be further decisions which were taken to set up a sub-committee consisting of Earl Grey, Sir Horace St Paul and Mr Hodgson to meet the proposed contractors in London for the purpose of finalising the start of construction, if terms could be negotiated. The firm concerned were Messrs Waring, a national firm of some repute, with considerable railway experience, for example in the construction of trunk lines like the Manchester, Sheffield and Lincolnshire Railway, later to become The Great Central(1). Why Warings, a London based firm, were approached is at no point clear, certainly they were in a higher league than Messrs Boulton Trowsdale & Son who were engaged upon the building of the Wansbeck Railway. One would surmise that the latter might have been interested enough to tender and win such a closely situated and similar contract. The reason may well be that Boulton Trowsdale & Son had two years work ahead of them with the Wansbeck Railway and were as heavily committed as they could be. There might have been more in the situation than that, however. They refused to work on the W.R unless Tone's powers were limited. They won their case against Tone and the Directors but the matter wasn't finally resolved until 1869. Secondly, during discussion it became apparent that, even at this early stage, the figures quoted showed the seriousness of the N.C.R's financial situation. Such was this as to cause the suggestion to be made on the first of numerous occasions that only the Scots Gap to Rothbury section should be pursued at that stage. It is nowhere apparent that any thought was given to the fact that these decisions were constitutionally irregular, nor to the trouble they might cause in the future.

Because of the local nature of sources of funds, qualification for directorship consisted merely in £500 being taken up in shares. The Board consisted of Earl Grey (Chairman); Sir Horace St Paul (Vice-chairman); John Bolam (Alwinton); George Culley (Fowberry); George Grey (Millfield); Richard Hodgson (Carham); Sir John Swinburne (Capheaton); Sir W.C Trevelyan (Wallington) and John Ord (Kelso), the latter the only representative from North of The Border. Benjamin Woodman, Morpeth solicitor and minor landowner at Stobhill was confirmed as company secretary and the auditors were William Forster (Rothbury) and Thomas Gow (Cambo). J.F.Tone, who had started life working on The Newcastle & North Shields Railway, was appointed engineer. He had only modest experience as a railway civil engineer, but had carried out work elsewhere in the country. His working life started when he was articled to his uncle, Robert Nicholson, becoming a junior partner. Nicholson was appointed engineer to the Border Counties Railway but died in 1855. The post did not automatically descend to Tone as junior partner and he had to re-apply, still a relatively inexperienced young man. His management did not leave a good record due to his insisting on late, quite major alterations to construction. This together with his dilatory issuing of completion certificates to the contractor, Hutchinson, must have been a major part of the latters financial problems and well known to Messrs Boulton Trowsdale & Son. However, Tone obviously wanted to settle back in the North-East. Perhaps the pull of his roots in Northumberland may have affected his career. As we know, he was involved with industry at Bellingham and did much work on Northumberland secondary lines. Probably he was capable, had he so chosen, of greater things, certainly his engineering management on the N.C.R appeared the equal of his successor, a national figure, G.B.Bruce, in the rivalries that lay ahead. His later dismissal was to become a matter of division in the camp, the row coming to a head in 1867.

As is so often the case, one interesting facet of the scene was who of The "County Set" were not members of The Board. For example, Ralph Carr-Ellison might have been expected to be present because his estate at Hedgley was likely to benefit substantially. The views of Lord Ravensworth and The Earl of Tankerville at this stage are not recorded. They seem likely to have been uncommitted and non-committal.

The second half-yearly shareholders meeting indicates the position with regard to the Hedgley Estate of Mr.J.Carr, an important mid-line site lying geographically between the northern and southern factions. The gloom which pervaded the chairman's opening speech with regard to progress, or rather the lack of it, was somewhat dispelled by his being able to quote a letter from Mr.Carr's solicitors, Messrs Dickson who had written from Alnwick on 10th August 1866 as follows;

Mr.Carr of Hedgley has shown us your two notices to take land (5a 1r 6p and 5a 2r 8p) from his estates of Hedgley and Prendwick. He feels well satisfied that the railway will be for the benefit of the county so that he empowers us to say that he will give the land to the company upon condition that they indemnify the tenants all damages, and make sure convenient access to, or crossings between the fields on each side of the railway as he may think necessary. As to compensating the tenants for the land abstracted, Mr.Carr will take that and all the severance damage upon himself.......[if the plans are altered], Mr.Carr must be again consulted and free to act as he may think right.

Yours truly,

W.W. & P.T.Dickson.

The Chairman stated that (the shareholders) would agree that this was a most liberal offer ("hear, hear") Eleven acres of good land at £200 per acre would be "the handsome present" of £2,200 towards completion of the work (applause). (And that did not take into account the compensation due to tenants mentioned in the latter - author)

Most important of all The Duke of Northumberland was positively against the scheme. Through Hugh Taylor, his estate commissioner, we find the statement: "The Duke is not disposed to interfere. In all probability the scheme will not go on for want of funds". Probably the 4th Duke and his advisers were shrewd enough to foresee trouble and felt it prudent not to risk getting burnt fingers, as had so nearly happened with their involvement in the Border Counties Railway. At that time The Dukes financial involvement had been saved by the fortuitous entry into affairs of the North British Board, a fact his advisors, men such as Hugh Taylor, would not forget. This may again have bearing on the sacking of Tone.

Nevertheless, early in 1864, The Directors were able to state that terms had been arranged for the purchase of land from Scots Gap Junction to Rothbury. This would largely be because Trevelyan was most keen to exploit the high quality limestone on his estate. With the exception of Coldstream, enthusiasm in the North seems to have been considerable (being led by Sir Horace St Paul of Ewart Park). It was the middle section of the planned route that appeared to present problems with regard to the purchase of land.

The proposals arising from the February 1864 meeting were

acted upon by April, in plenty of time for the half yearly meeting of shareholders on 9th August. The Secretary (Benjamin Woodman) read out the advertisement convening the meeting and read the report of the directors:

"The Directors report that work had not actually yet commenced. The amount of capital had however been so nearly subscribed, which will allow them to call upon the contractors to complete simultaneously the two sections, Cornhill-Wooler and Scots Gap-Rothbury. A call of £2 per share would be made at an early date, the sum required for this purpose has actually been obtained; there was a deficiency on subscriptions of £2000 to be raised under a recent public act, on security of rent charges on estates benefited by the railway, a portion only will be immediately available for work and current expenses.... It is to be hoped that a considerable proportion of the capital required to construct the intermediate portion between Rothbury and Wooler will be derived from this source......the cost of staking out the line in preparation of land notices and the salaries of officials are the only liabilities". A letter from J.F Tone about staking was then read out. This indicated completion from Scots Gap to Tosson and Mile Moor near Whittingham to Cornhill (of the 36.5 miles some 23 3/8ths had been completed.) He also indicated that the earthworks required were a little less in quantity than were those in the parliamentary estimate.

An agreement was reached to modify the contract so that construction could begin with the working capital reduced from £65,000 to £50,000 in paid up shares(2) But even this more modest target became the basis of dispute between the company and the contractors, the latter remaining unconvinced of the viability by virtue of raising funds from the Lands Improvement Company. This is understandable in that it was a new form of investment and had never been applied to a railway. It is hard to agree with Jenkins "(that) the Northumberland Central project had made a good start"(3). For instance we find that at the next meeting The Terminable Annuities Act, by which much store had been set, had not affected the N.C.R share situation. Shares were selling only slowly, no construction work was under way and, in fact, the Company was £1500 short of the agreed figure which would allow a start to be made. The contractors, Messrs Warings, as was common practice at the time, agreed to take £8,630 in shares(4) These were of course worthless

The 1861 Alnwick Proposal

Sketch taken from a map held in the Swinburne
papers deposited in the NRO. This shows:

_____ proposed railway from Alnwick to Wooler
avoiding Hulme Park and the Hillhead ridge

========= proposed Northern extension to Yetholm and Kelso

 Hatched area indicates where this proposed line
differed from the Northumberland Central 1863 route
and the 1881 Alnwick - Cornhill route of the NSR

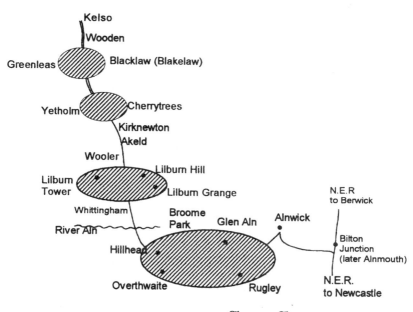

signed: *Thomas Thompson*
Thomas Thompson
Surveyor
Alnwick 1861

until either cash from working profits could flow into the contractor's accounts, or subscriptions from other sources were such that the Waring shares could be sold. Warings were rightly cautious in that they had obligations to the Lands Improvement Co. and the Exchequer as well as the N.C.R. For the Exchequer they had responsibilities under the 8% (£20,800), deposit arrangement into the Court of Chancery, which were forfeit if the company did not raise 50% of its capital under The Act. (Warings share was approximately one third). The Lands Improvement Company, incorporated in 1853, had its amendment allowing loans to railways granted only in 1859. The reimbursement of individual landowners would only take place after the line had been constructed. Whilst this repayment would come largely from anticipated rent increases from improved access to land e.g. for lime, and improved transport of livestock and crops with the possibility of materials at favourable prices for the construction of roads, buildings and drainage, it did not allow for land purchase or initial construction work on the trackbed. In order to avoid the necessity of withdrawing The Bill in accord with this stipulation, and thereby sacrificing the whole of the money which had been sunk in the preliminary expenses. The Directors entered into an agreement with Messrs Waring...(who) undertook to release the sum deposited in the Court of Chancery by the Lands Improvement Company by making themselves responsible to the Treasury to the amount for the due prosecution of the railway under the contract of 23rd June 1863.

The main items of this agreement were:-
1.That the contractors would repay to the Lands Improvement Co the Exchequer Bills of £20,800 deposited with the Court of Chancery.

2.That the Railway Co would concur in all measures to procure repayment to the contractors.

3.That the Railway Co would use its best endeavours to complete the subscription of capital.

4 That the Contractors when in possession of the land required....in consideration of the payment by the company at the time, and in the manner above-mentioned of £280,000 ...by the parties of the first part (The Directors) and the Company of the Acts, conditions and stipulations on their part to be observed and performed, would execute

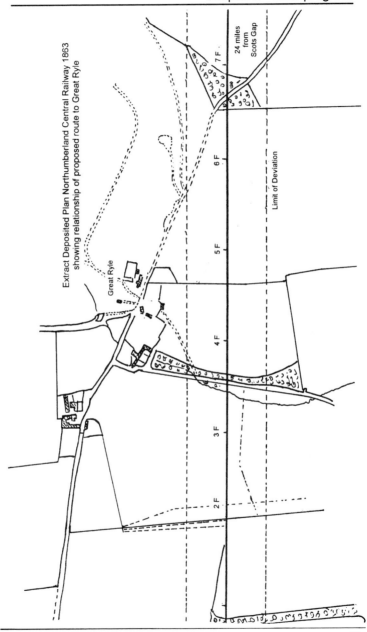

Extract Deposited Plan Northumberland Central Railway 1863 showing relationship of proposed route to Great Ryle

Great Ryle

24 miles from Scots Gap

7 F

6 F

5 F

4 F

3 F

2 F

Limit of Deviation

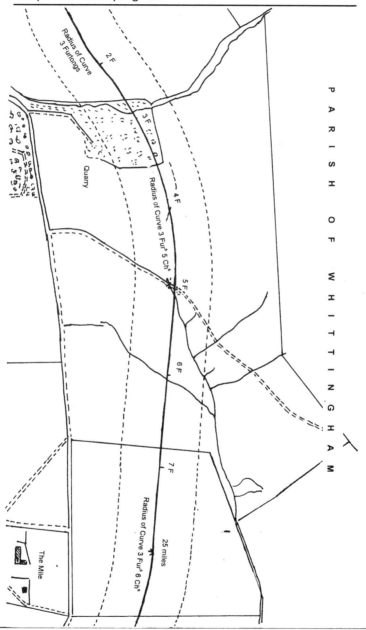

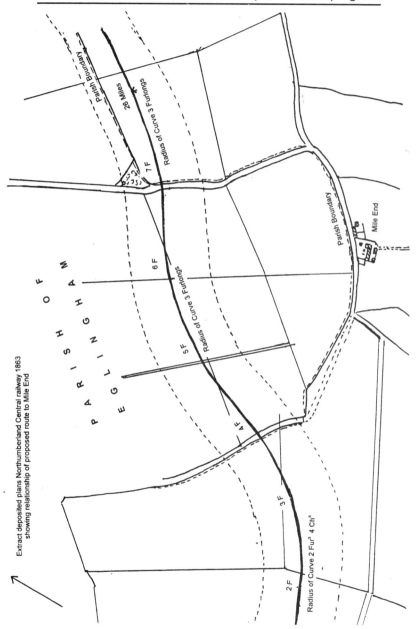

Extract deposited plans Northumberland Central railway 1863 showing relationship of proposed route to Mile End

PARISH OF EGLINGHAM

Parish Boundary

26 Miles

Radius of Curve 3 Furlongs

7 F

6 F

5 F

Radius of Curve 3 Furlongs

4 F

3 F

2 F

Radius of Curve 2 Fur^s 4 Ch^s

Parish Boundary

Mile End

the works according to the plans and specifications prepared or approved by J.F.Tone Esq, the Engineer of the Company, and would provide stations etc to the amount not exceeding £10,000. (Thus the basis upon which the Company's loan was used appears to have been illegal, though there appears to have been no recorded test case in the courts).

5.If the Company should not construct the Coldstream Junction to Coldstream branch, a proportionate reduction in the contract sum be made.

6.The Company shall find all land and, within 12 months of passing of the Act to put the Contractors in possession of so much as would enable them to commence.

7.The work to be completed within the period mentioned in The Act.

8.The Company to pay the Contractors the £280,000 as to £90,000 in shares and as to £190,000 in cash by monthly instalments.

9.Powers to be provided for the Engineer to extend the time for completion.

10.The Company to confirm the agreement under their seal within 3 months of passing the Act.

11.The personal liability of the directors to cease.

Modifications made at the Meeting on 24th February 1864 were:

1.If £40,000 became available, the line to Rothbury from Scots Gap should be commenced.

2.If £65,000 was available work on both the Northern and Southern sections to commence. In April 1864 the £65,000 clause was reduced to £50,000.

3.Shares of the Contractors to be taken up in the course of construction. In the event of the company stopping short of completion of the whole railway the proportion of shares to be held by the contractors shall be readjusted by the Engineer so as to bear the same ratio as £90,000 bears to £280,000.

The August 1864 meeting ended with a informal whip-round which raised the required £1500!(5), a cheering prospect. Not all was doom and gloom. From far away Simla in the Indian Hill Country, Sir W Trevelyan wrote to W Calverley Trevelyan on 12th August 1864. *"I write with pleasure to give such help as I am able to the Northumberland Central Railway. On 1st Sept I will remit to Messrs Drummond £500 and another £500 on 1st October. Both to be invested in the N.C.R. Mr Woodman, the secretary has written to me saying that he had sent me a prospectus and form of application for shares. But, as they have not arrived, you will perhaps be so kind as to let my son-in-law, Harry Holland, who manages such affairs for me, know where the £1000 is to be paid"* (6).

The early months of 1865 were critical to the Northumberland Central Railway. Moore(7) presents a summary of the effects of the Land Clauses Consolidation Act of 1864 (arising subsequent to a House of Lords Committee meeting in the previous year). We have discussed earlier how this was intended to work. He gives three reasons for its failure. First some landholders paid fixed rents (presumably long-term agreements). The N.C.R attempts to get round these failed. Secondly, other tenants could hardly be expected to pay higher rents voluntarily no matter how much their land (allegedly) benefited, if this could be avoided, or at least prolonged by lengthy negotiation. Finally, and of considerable interest, some tenants, especially those with short leases, were worried that their landlords did not support the railway(8). This applied, for example, to tenants of the 4th Duke who was so unconvinced of the beneficial effects of the railway that he refused to even consider raising rents. Others who were prepared to do so, may have left the required infrastructure severely alone, in which case a tenant willing to have his rent raised might have found very little advantage gained.

The meeting in February 1865 was held at The White Swan, Alnwick, with Sir Horace St Paul in the chair. Clearly the hope was that a new venue might generate new interest, particularly from within the ranks of the Alnwick competitors. A £2 call on shares was made in order to make the £50,000 necessary to commence construction. This was hardly encouraged by the answer given to a shareholder who enquired as to the interest on existing money which had been banked. This was to the effect that, owing to an oversight, it was earning nothing. In defence, Hodgson promised to look into the matter immediately after the meeting. This same meeting saw a dispute as to where construction should actually commence, an issue which with hindsight would seem to be crucial. However, the fact was that no decision had been taken and the meeting was split three ways. One view was for starting at each end simultaneously. In view of the financial state this must be regarded as glorious optimism. The Wooler end had the easier terrain and the promise of quicker returns, being said to cost £35,000. Its merit was that it served a relatively rich agricultural area which would use any portion of the line (whether to Wooler or not) as soon as it was constructed. Its disadvantage lay in connection with the N.E.R which remained aloof and unfriendly, if not actually hostile. The Southern end, at an estimated £50,000 would not only cost more but virtually have to wait until Rothbury was reached before becoming economically effective, but at least it connected with a co-operative railway in co-operative territory.

Mr Hodgson-Hinde said there had been a 40% call-up and not a spade in the ground! He wanted to know why nothing had been done. The explanation given was far from satisfactory.

The Directors only then disclosed the financial arrangements which had been reached with the contractors (£28,000 allowed a start at the north end, and £48,000 a start at the south; the £65000 for a start at both ends clearly being beyond reach). But they disclosed much more. They stated that on 25th August 1864, the Company, being in a position to perform their part of the agreement, The Secretary gave notice to The Contractors, but in the absence of Mr Charles Waring, no definite reply was received until 6th October, when, in a letter from their law agent, the first intimation was given to the Company of the desire on the part of Warings to avoid fulfilling their several agreements, as had been understood by The Directors. Lengthy correspondence ensued (of which we have no details, but it is easy to see Waring's concern in the relationship of the financial plight to the original contract, and, in particular the modifications of 24th February 1864, as outlined above.)

Under these circumstances, the meeting was told that The Directors had obtained the legal opinion and services of Mr Lloyd in chambers and the case submitted to him for counsel's opinion. The specific points raised were:

1.Whether the original contract and supplementary modifications were legally binding on the contractors.
2.What were the obligations on the contractors to commence and complete the two sections.
3.What was the effect of the non-delivery of land within the 12 calendar months of the passing of the Act.
4.What course should the company pursue.
5.If the company deem it advisable, how might they free themselves from the contractors and the contract.
6.What, if any, liability will attach to the company in the event of re-letting the work.
7.Generally to advise upon the relative position of the two parties.

Mr Lloyd had given his opinion as follows:

1.I am of the opinion that the original contract became binding on the Contractors, but [as to] the supplementary [1864 modifications] they are morally and in honour binding. I do not think the performance of them could be enforced against the contractors by any proceedings at law or in equity.
I very much doubt that anything effectual could be done [with regard to both the original agreement and the supplementary]
2.I consider the fair effect of the whole arrangement that the Contractors will execute and complete the whole of the undertaking as divided into three sections.
3.I am of the opinion that the obligation to deliver the land within the twelve months has been by mutual consent dispensed with. As respect of the monthly payments, or rather the principle on which they are made, by agreement with the Contractors and Engineer, I do not find the supplementary agreement at all affects this part of the contract.
4.My opinion is that the Company and the Contractors are both powerless in any adverse proceedings.
5.Practically therefore there is no appreciable risk to the company re-letting the works.
6.I cannot but think that the demurs of the contractors are mainly due to the state of the money market. I suggest a meeting of the parties in my chambers.

Railways of Northumberland 1865 - 6

Completed   ———

Under construction or proposed ············

1	N.B.R Edinburgh - Berwick
2	N.E.R Newcastle - Berwick
3	Blyth & Tyne Railway
4	B & T.R Lough Bridge Branch
5	Proposed South Northumberland Railway (Original Scheme)
6	Scotswood and Scots Gap Railway
7	Wansbeck Valley Railway
8	Newcastle and Carlisle (N.E.R)
9	Allendale Branch
10	Alston Branch (N.E.R)
11	Border Counties (N.B.R)
12	Waverley Route (N.B.R)
13	Jedburgh Branch (N.B.R)
14	Berwick and Kelso (N.E.R)
15	Alnwick Branch (N.E.R)
16	Northumberland Central Railway

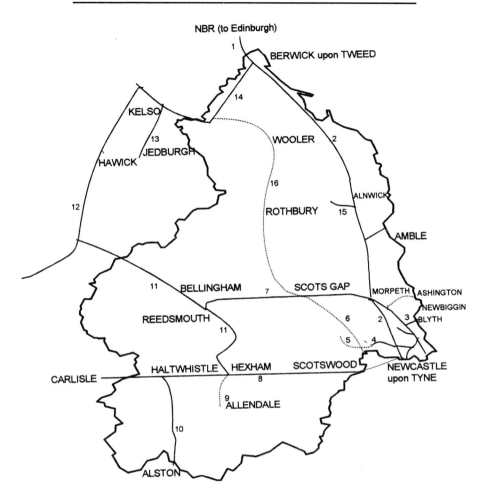

NBR (to Edinburgh)

1

BERWICK upon TWEED

14

KELSO

13
JEDBURGH

HAWICK

WOOLER   2

16

12

ROTHBURY   15

ALNWICK

AMBLE

11   BELLINGHAM   7   SCOTS GAP

MORPETH   ASHINGTON

NEWBIGGIN

REEDSMOUTH   6   2   3   BLYTH

11

5   4

HALTWHISTLE   HEXHAM   SCOTSWOOD   NEWCASTLE
upon TYNE

CARLISLE   8

9
ALLENDALE

10

ALSTON

The directors adopted this last recommendation. There were several meetings and the result was the expressed determination of Mr Waring on the part of himself and his partnership not to carry out the undertakings to which they had agreed.

Counsel's further opinion was that Messrs Warings were not inclined to proceed with the work...and are desirous of obtaining some personal guarantee or other security for payment of the contract price....the only course open to the promoters is to treat the arrangements with Messrs Warings as at an end. I repeat that both parties are practically powerless as respect of any proceedings. Messrs Warings may, and probably will, unless released from their liability in the manner of the deposit, threaten, and even initiate proceedings by way of an injunction or otherwise.....It would be expedient to buy off the litigation and annoyance by relieving Messrs Waring from their liability.

Richard Hodgson explained further that the sum of £280,000 had been signed by the directors and sealed, and part of the contract was for the company's engineer to lay out the line in the most economical way. Later with the whole capital not subscribed certain sections had been staked out. The contractors had said "these are not sufficient for us. We must be guided in our bond by the works we are to make on the whole; we must have the whole of the working plans from beginning to end". Expense and delay was the result. He believed the contractors were now perfectly satisfied. This was the first difference and the second was with regard to payments. Subscriptions were not coming in to meet the whole of the line. He then reiterated the figures for portions of the line [as outlined earlier]. He thought they could procure £50,000 and had asked the contractors to commence. Warings had however written to Mr Woodman to say that the documents were not formal. There was disagreement over the 12 month clause, with regard to the handing over of land, The company said it must stick to monthly payments for work done, and they thought it possible to obtain better contracts elsewhere than with Warings.

Hodgson-Hinde proposed an amendment to this report; "That the report now read be received; and that the thanks of this meeting be given to the directors for the attention they have paid to the interests of shareholders, especially in reference to the contracts entered into, but, at the same time, this meeting views with alarm the prospect of litigation to enforce the performance of such contracts against unwilling parties". After much discussion this was seconded by Mr Forster.

Richard Hodgson said it was a censure of the directors. He would give his seat to anyone supporting the amendment. Eventually a modified report was found acceptable but with much bad grace.

The Directors indicated that they had decided it was best not to adopt proceedings to compel Messrs Warings to fulfill their contract. They proposed to take measures to construct the line without their assistance, commencing with the section of line from Scots Gap to Rothbury. Certain landowners are contemplating the construction of a line in the neighbourhood of Wooler into Scotland via the Kail Water. If this project should be carried into effect, it may probably render it expedient to modify their intended line North of Wooler.

The re-election took place of Earl Grey(Chairman), Sir Horace St Paul, Sir W.Trevelyan and Mr. R Hodgson.

Sir Horace St Paul thought the N.B.R had insidious designs in view in a wish to appropriate the N.C.R but Richard Hodgson pointed out that the N.B.R and possibly the N.E.R were in competition with the N.C.R. He said that it was his personal interest to construct the north end of the line and the N.B.R (of which he was chairman) "never had art nor part of the scheme". Mr Ord of Nisbet, Kelso,said he had taken on himself to approach the N.B.R for support of a scheme from "Jedburgh or Kelso to the area of N.C.R" but was told "the line would be injurious to the N.B.R". These statements appear to have influenced the meeting into the belief that Sir Horace St Paul's view was erroneous. However, it can surely be argued that any competitive predator would take advantage of the weak financial position of the N.C.R to swallow it up, perhaps with modifications after injection of cash, to suit its own purposes.

The directors were still confident of a 4% return on a line costing less than £5000 per mile. This bold statement to which the signature of Grey was appended as chairman, can hardly have carried conviction and the decision to move the venue of this meeting into rival territory must have been more of a disaster than a success.

A month before the next half-yearly meeting, Warings acted, regardless of the legal niceties being settled and asked to be relieved of their contract from July 3rd. In the words of Sewell "they had simply had enough"(9). The sombre thoughts of potential litigation would still hang over the railway but at least, the air had been cleared prior to the next meeting.

This, the fourth half-yearly meeting on 7th August 1865 was again held at The White Swan, Alnwick, Earl Grey being in the chair. He faced angry shareholders with the news that no start had been made. It was clear to all that hard decisions could no longer be postponed. He put it bluntly that the choice was abandonment unless some agreement could be forged with Messrs Warings, for this would mean the forfeiture of the £28,800 deposited. The Railway Times(10) reporting the Chairman's speech listed the problems, which must have been obvious to all present, that the contractors were unwilling to start until the previously mentioned financial dispute had been settled, but that greater support from landowners was required, whom he said had "blighted" the proposed railway; he thought that they had a right to "expect" that support because of "the extreme importance of railway communication to the districts which were at a disadvantage" compared with districts which had a railway....the line would bring together two parts of the district, in one of which coal and lime were abundant, and in the other deficient, and so it would be to the mutual advantage of both."

Much more serious was the Warings debacle. He indicated that in the existing financial situation no other contractor was likely to be willing to continue. The forfeiture of the £28,800 was glossed over with regard to its contentious use of Lands Improvement Co. funding.

The chairman stated that enough money was available to build as far as Rothbury at the southern end. It was resolved both to do this and accept Waring's request. Tone was left as the sole outside officer of the company with Woodman as secretary. The Chairman appealed for loyalty from the shareholders, implying that otherwise the Board would resign. The report was seconded by Sir John Swinburne but Sir Horace St Paul immediately followed with another of his swashbuckling speeches stating how painful it was for him to disagree with his fellow directors but he felt that the money should be available for the northern end. Although he had an interest in that his estate was at Ewart Park, north of Wooler, this did make economic sense, as already suggested (The Northern section was about half the cost of the Southern). He spoilt his case by proposing that building should nevertheless commence at both ends, but he did not indicate how he would have financed this.

Richard Hodgson proposed a compromise solution in which the meeting would agree to start construction at the southern end, but publicly disclaim any intention to abandon any part of the line and construct the northern section as early as circumstances would permit. When the southern section was completed and opened to traffic, funds for the northern section would be raised by the issue, if required of preference shares. This was astute. It placated the northern shareholders (who, as we know, were a majority) yet, here could be seen the Chairman of the North British Railway beating his chest at some future date and then magically calling upon the N.B.R to extricate the N.C.R from the financial mess in which it had found itself by the injection of capital, even though the local shares had not been fully taken up, a situation we have already encountered on the Border Counties Railway. The softening up process prior to absorbing a sprat in order to turn it into part of a trunk-line mackerel was under way (even if he had once again, earlier in the meeting, announced that he was acting in an individual capacity). This composite motion was broken down into the first part, carried unanimously and the second, defeated by nine votes to five(11). The meeting offered the contract to a local man, Mr Dowson, but he had sub-contractors to begin the Scots Gap-Rothbury section at four points at a total sum of £44,258, this being seen as a way of speeding up the processes of construction, improving the cash flow problems and shortening the interval between the start and revenue returns from the southern section.

Earl Grey wrote long letters to Trevelyan and Ralph Carr-Ellison from the Morpeth offices of the N.C.R on 30th November 1865, and to a number of other individuals. These were all very similar in content and, after customary preambles concerning the need of the railway and local enthusiasm, he wrote;

"The amount of capital hitherto subscribed is barely sufficient to complete the southern section of the line which is now in progress

from Scots Gap to Rothbury and if more capital cannot be raised, the Railway must stop short at Rothbury, leaving the larger and more important part of the District still to suffer from the want of a better means of communication. There is no hope now that the additional capital can be obtained except by the assistance of those interested in the property of the district through which the railway has to pass ...if completed it must confidently be expected to yield a fair interest for their money to shareholders.[But] It does not hold out a sufficient prospect of high profit to afford a temptation for mere speculative investment...." He went on to repeat the description of the Lands Improvement Co. scheme "which would mean no risk to locally invested capital". He described the main snag of this scheme being that landowners might pay increased charges and tenants get the most benefit, and repeated the problem of the grants only becoming available on completion. The Northumberland Central Railway had therefore caused a form of agreement to be prepared by which tenants should bind themselves to pay rent charges on their farms during the continuance of their occupation to such an amount as might be considered proper in each case, provided the landlords on their side would undertake to avail themselves of the power conferred upon them by the Law to raise money for the railway and would also consent that their tenants should be entitled to such a proportion of the shares as might be paid for them during the continuation of their tenure(12). It was a last desperate plea.

The fifth half-yearly meeting, again in Alnwick on 28th February 1866 had "not a numerous attendance of shareholders". Mr Hodgson was in the chair. It contained the report of the directors on the Waring negotiations. The contract had been given to Mr Dowson at a sum of £44,498 0s 7d. exclusive of materials for permanent way. Up to 31st January 1866 £1,761 had been expended mainly on surveys and promotion etc. To proceed with the southern section meant" disappointment" in quarters where the northern section was held to be more important. £3,200 had been given in shares in lieu of land but some was not yet available for construction (in reply to a question by Mr Hodgson-Hinde). The Chairman said the Company had entered into contracts for £42,500 and they had just got that amount of share capital for the purpose. Mr Hodgson-Hinde replied; "Yes, if you can get your share capital." The Chairman said that in addition they had materials to pay for - between £15,000 and £16,000. The obligations came to £61,500 with a subscribed capital of £42,000. He still expected a fair dividend and the Scots Gap-Rothbury section to be completed in 12 months. However those present at the meeting do not seem to have been greatly impressed with the situation.

And with that the shareholders had to be content. They cannot have been happy about the prospects of litigation still looming, apart from the parlous finances and the decisions to build the hardest thirteen miles, covering territory backed by the least number of investors.

Scots Gap Station

CENTRAL NORTHUMBERLAND RAILWAY.

CAPITAL £260,000 IN 26,000 SHARES OF £10 EACH.
Deposit, £1 5s. per Share.

EXECUTIVE COMMITTEE.

THE EARL GREY.
RICHARD HODGSON, Esq., M.P., Carham.
GEORGE ANNETT GREY, Esq., Milfield.
SIR W. C. TREVELYAN, Bart., Wallington.
JOHN GREY, Esq., Dilston.
GEORGE CULLEY, Esq., Fowberry.
SIR HORACE ST. PAUL, Bart., Ewart.
THOMAS GOW, Esq., Cambo.

THE EARL OF DURHAM.
T. MASON, Esq., Fallinsburn.
WALTER JOHNSON, Esq., Trench Hall, Gateshead.
J. ORDE, Esq., Howtel.
WALTER SELBY, Esq., Biddleston.
FAIRFAX FEARNLEY, Esq., Adderstone House.
W. LYNN SMART, Esq., Trewhitt House.
W. A. BECK, Esq., Cartington.
The Rev T. ILDERTON, Felton.

THE CHAIRMAN AND VICE-CHAIRMAN OF EACH LOCAL COMMITTEE.

LOCAL COMMITTEES.

COLDSTREAM.

W. CUNNINGHAM, Coldstream, Chairman.
W. NICHOLSON, Lennel Hill, Vice-chairman.
Sir J. MARJORIBANKS, Bart., of Lees.
D. ROBERTSON, Esq., M.P., Ladykirk.
J. MILNE HOME, Esq., of Wedderburn.
J. HOOD, of Stoneridge.
M. D. HUNTER, of Antonshill.
G. WILSON, of Gleegerfield.
J. CUNNINGHAM, Coldstream.
W. DOUGLAS, Coldstream.
A. SCOTT, Glen Douglas.
T. HOGG, Coldstream
T. HOOD, Coldstream Mains.
M. J. TURNBULL, M.D., Coldstream.
R. TAIT, Lees Mill.
J. HALLIBURTON, Coldstream.
T. MELROSE, Coldstream.
R. CARMICHAEL, Coldstream.
R. HENDERSON, Coldstream.
A. FISH, Coldstream.
W. STAMFORD, Coldstream.
W. HUTCHISON, jun., Ruthom.

WOOLER.

C. REA, Doddington, Chairman.
C. SELBY, Yearle, Vice-chairman.
J. ALEXANDER, Wooler.
W. JOHNSON, Turrelaws.
W. WIGHTMAN, Wooler.
J. BOYD, Doddington.
J. GREY, Kimmerston.
R. KING, Wooperton.
J. BROWN, Wooler.
Rev. J. S. GREEN, Wooler.
J. D. BELL, Wooler.
J. D. CLARK, Ilderton.
G. P. HUGHES, Middleton Hall.

ALN VALE.

T. FORSTER, Screnwood, Chairman.
H. SCOTT, Alnham, Vice-chairman
Rev. R. W. GOODENOUGH, Whittingham.
Rev. G. S. THOMPSON, Alnham
Rev. T. ORD, Callaly.
H. CRISP, Prendwick.
W. THOMPSON, Little Ryle.
W. COLVILLE, Yetlington.
J. PATTISON, Crosshill.
J. STEPHENSON, Thrunton.
J. COULL, Rothill.
T. HUDSON, Glanton.
J. ATKINSON, Brandon.
R. COWLEY, Mountain.
G. DRYSDALE, Ryle.
G. BOLAM, jun., Hedgeley.
K. DONKIN, Glanton.
J. GRAY, Titlington.
J. TURNBULL, Branton.
W. COULSON, Ellingham Newtown.
R. S. STOREY, Beanley.

COQUET VALE.

W. FORSTER, Burradon, Chairman.
J. BOLAM, Alwinton, Vice-chairman.
Rev. A. PROCTER, Alwinton.
C. R. ILDERTON, Tosson.
E. PRINGLE, Snitter.
T. ALLEN, Snitter.
J. AYNSLEY, Raw.
R. CARR, Hirst.
T. S. STOREY, Ellaw.
G. MILBURN, Rothbury.
E. TEMPLE, Rothbury.
A. ORD, Lindsrels.
C. YOUNG, Puncherton.
J. BOLAM, Trewhitt.
T. HENDERSON, Warton.
T. CUMMINGS, Newtown.
T. CUMMINGS, Rothbury.
W. FORSTER, jun., Burradon.
J. BOLAM, Bickerton.
G. CRAWFORD, Cartington.
A. ROBERTSON, Peels.
W. BELL, Thropton.
H. WHITFIELD, Harbottle.

ENGINEER.
J. F. TONE, NEWCASTLE-UPON-TYNE.

PARLIAMENTARY AGENTS.
MESSRS. PRITT, SHERWOOD, VENABLES, GRUBBE, AND JONES, 7, GREAT GEORGE STREET, WESTMINSTER, LONDON, S.W.

SOLICITOR AND SECRETARY.
BENJAMIN WOODMAN, MORPETH.

TREASURERS AND BANKERS.
W. H. LAMBTON AND CO., NEWCASTLE-UPON-TYNE.

BROKERS.
LONDON—
NEWCASTLE-UPON-TYNE—
EDINBURGH—
GLASGOW—
MANCHESTER—

Chapter 6

1866 and all that

We must now leave the N.C.R and its meetings in Morpeth and Alnwick and turn our attention to the economy of the nation, which was to hit the N.C.R hard. By 1864 the financial screw was tightening in that the heyday of the railway entrepreneurs was largely over, money less forthcoming, and investment in railway infrastructure was largely in the hands of the Banks. By the next year, the Bank of England was tightening its fiscal policies and finance companies were resisting contractors and directors demands. Bank rate rose to 10%. As ever, the construction industry was quickly hit, investors nationally were increasingly nervous and the accelerating spiral downwards caused the failure of bankers Overend and Gurney, who were particularly involved in loans to railway contractors. The Bank Charter Act was suspended and a major depression arose in 1866 which, after developing with frightening speed, was slow to recover. Thus small businesses like the N.C.R were unable to borrow except on crippling terms - if at all(1).

North of The Border, we need to consider the North British Railway, where angry and suspicious shareholders mounted an attack on The Board, and particularly the Chairman, who, of course, was Richard Hodgson. Hodgson had against the advice of his staff, insisted on a 3% dividend. John Walker, a newly appointed officer of the company, found the accounts "too good to be true". He reported this to two directors, John and Ronald Beaumont, but, at a Board meeting when this was investigated, Hodgson weathered the storm. James White of Overtoun, a shareholder, heard rumours of this and other irregularities and requested an enquiry. (He was a man of substance and some power, being chairman of the Glasgow & South Western Railway, proprietor of the Rutherglen Chemical Factory and Chairman of the National Bible Society of Scotland. He also was a strict sabbatarian and had already clashed heavily with Hodgson because the N.B.R policy was to run trains on Sundays)(2).

Hodgson had inherited some of his problems. The N.B.R promoters had talked about 8% dividends and many shareholders had been looking for this. In fact, the dividend was never greater than 5% (1848) and in 1851, 1852 and 1853 had been nil. The problem all railways faced was that reserves of capital were anathema to investors, yet capital expenditure was by the nature of railway expansion "lumpy"(3). After the railway mania, market prices tended to fall below par so that investors felt the need for quick returns. Eventually a committee of eight N.B.R shareholders produced a report and summed the situation up as " a careful and most ingenious fabrication of imaginary accounts had been perpetrated". By charging over £300,000 to the capital account, instead of from revenue for at least three and a half years, the books had been systematically cooked...to exhibit an ability to pay the particular dividend desired by Mr Hodgson(4). The outcome was the publication of a notice on 21st May 1867 "To Holders of Guaranteed and Preference Stocks of the North British Railway" by W.M. Wilkinson, Solicitors of Lincoln's Inn Fields, London, of a lengthy statement of the financial situation. A summary would be that the loss to preference shareholders was £1,875,000 and to ordinary stockholders £437,000. Hodgson tried to hang on, but no man could face figures as daunting as these. In poor health and no longer the force-majeur of former days, Hodgson resigned to continue his railway activities where he could, and particularly with his Northumberland railway interests. By now he was a broken and bitter man. We can sense the ripples hitting the periphery in correspondence between Sir Walter Trevelyan and Calverley Trevelyan;

To Calverley:
8th.November 1868
8 Grosvenor Crescent;

"...the state of finances of the N.B.R will not I hope make any difference in the branches in which you are interested. I have just paid the last installment of my contribution of £1000 to the Rothbury branch"

and on 17th.December 1866.

"The resolution sent to me relating the Central Railway(sic) has been skillfully drawn up and will I hope lead at no distant period to the extension of the line north and south through the whole length of the County and this is, I presume, Sir J. Swinburne's doing".

and on 25th.October 1867 from Nettlecombe;

"I duly received the circular addressed to the shareholders of the N.C.R. My reason for not answering it was that the position has been entirely altered by the arrangement last proposed [see below], and has been put upon the footing of an ordinary investment by the issue of new shares at the rate which entitles the holder to twice the profits derivable from the old shares. Although the form is different, the principle and the practical effect are precisely the same as if the new issue consisted of preference shares. At a considerable personal sacrifice I contributed £1000 towards the construction of the railway and I do not object to my interest being postponed in the manner proposed if it is the necessity for the purpose of raising funds for the completion of the railway, but I am not prepared to make fresh investments which may be equally made by any person who wishes to get a fair rate of interest on his money.

What I have done, I think, is precisely what you did in reference to the Watchet Railway - to subscribe £1000 towards the undertaking but to decline to take part in the subsequent raising of money by the grant of preferential investment" (5).

The Northumberland Central Railway could hardly be in greater financial difficulties anyway, but its directors stuck to their guns, even though, for example, Sir Arthur Monck told Sir John Swinburne in September; "The capitalists have had time to recover from the panic. When they have recovered, they may turn their attention again to railways". Construction commenced in fact, in 1866, starting at Scots Gap, with sub-contractors working northwards. A meeting, held at Rothbury in October, appointed new members to The Board to make a further attempt to raise money from landowners. Algernon, 4th Duke of Northumberland, had died in 1865 and was succeeded by his cousin, George, whose tenure of the title was so short that he had little time to make an impact on the local economy. He, in turn, was succeeded by Algernon, 6th Duke, who immediately reversed the lukewarm attitude of his predecessors to the local economy, including the railway, although the financial benefits did not begin to filter through until the following year. Indeed, Lord Percy wrote to Sir Walter Trevelyan from Alnwick Castle on 10th October 1866, stating:

"after the most careful consideration of the arguments[placed] upon me at our last meeting, I have arrived at the conclusion that I

shall not be justified in recommending the Duke of Northumberland to make advances required for the completion of the portion of the Northumberland Central line now in progress between Scots Gap and Rothbury in the absence of any certainty that it would be carried out as to afford a complete communication between The Borders and Newcastle via Scotswood, including the town of Alnwick, in the accommodation to be enjoyed"

The Alnwick Castle view was clearly that the policy should be 'all or none' of the old concept of the through central route. It took the new Duke time to alter this view.

The minutes of the Director's meeting held at Morpeth on 18th.December 1866 included the following:

1. No details of the offer of His Grace the Duke of Northumberland by Lord Percy to meet His Graces wishes with respect to a Railway from Cornhill to Newcastle [are to hand] but it is not necessary to take steps for applying to Parliament for powers to alter and extend the line of the Northumberland Central Railway until a careful examination has been made of the details of the scheme suggested by Earl Percy and until such addition to their subscription list has been obtained.

2. The directors are compelled to advise shareholders of the Northumberland Central Railway to apply to parliament in the ensuing session for a Bill enabling them to abandon north of Rothbury and for the execution of which they have in vain endeavoured to obtain the necessary capital.

3.The shareholders having adopted this advice, a Bill has been prepared accordingly, Scots Gap to Rothbury will soon be completed leaving it open for future consideration in what manner it may hereafter be best extended both to the north and to the south.

4. The directors believe the railway to be most desirable it should be extended in both directions so as to form a continuous railway communication through Central Northumberland and between Newcastle and Cornhill with the least practical delay.

5. That the directors are ready to co-operate with the

landowners and others interested in carrying into effect the extensions of any other existing railway company who prefer to act independently, the Directors will be equally ready to afford them every facility and assistance in their power(6).

So, 1866, the year of many a crisis nationally, ended for the N.C.R, with a letter from Woodman to the shareholders and landowners following the above directors meeting as follows;

Northumberland Central Railway Act (1867)

I beg to inform you that application is intended to be made to parliament in the next session for the Act under the above title whereby it is proposed amongst other things, to authorise the Northumberland Central Railway Company to relinquish or abandon their construction and maintenance of all or part of the Northumberland Central Railway authorised by The Northumberland Central Railway Act of 1863, as lies northward of a certain point or place in the parish of Rothbury, shown on the plans and sections of the Northumberland Central Railway deposited with the Clerk of the the Peace of the County of Northumberland in the year 1862.

In the event of the proposed abandonment not being sanctioned, application will be made for the insertion in the intended Act of provision to extend the time limited by The Northumberland Central Railway Act of 1863 for the purchase of land etc [followed by a list of their properties affected to each landowner].

February 1867 saw the half-yearly meeting, with Sir Horace St Paul in the chair, abandoned through lack of a quorum. However the financial situation was disclosed at the request of Sir John Swinburne. Receipts were £9,677 12s 8d from all sources; expenditure £10,816 17s 10d, leaving a balance of £2,700 14s 0d(7). Woodman sent out a circular letter to landowners and shareholders on March 14th, saying that £39,000 had been expended on works. To complete them £40,000 was required. The directors had no personal interest in the section of line to Rothbury,[within the meaning of the Act] but if those having a proprietary interest [which did include others as well as directors] will subscribe an additional £32,000, the Directors will then exercise their borrowing powers to raise the deficiency of £20,000, so that, if the subscriptions are thus increased, there will be a certainty of the line being opened to traffic. If this is not done by 10th April, work will be suspended. The landowners whose property is intersected by or at a terminus of the line will lose the great advantage they would desire from its completion, and the subscription of the present shareholders will be entirely sacrificed. It remains therefore for the landowners and shareholders to decide".

The ultimate taking up of shares to the tune of £13,860 by the Duke in the summer of 1867 and announced at the August half-yearly meeting of shareholders clearly came in the nick of time, for since April all capital was exhausted and work suspended. The Duke's cash investment simply meant that work which had been suspended could re-start. The Bill to abandon north of Rothbury became law under The Northumberland Central Railway Act of 12th April 1867. The company was required to cancel the unsold shares, thus reducing the authorised capital to £75,000, with borrowing powers at a mere £25,000. This was followed by a meeting held on 30th April at Rothbury Court House with Sir W.B Riddell Bt of Hepple in the chair. The meeting was formally given details of the new Act, indicating that £5000 was anticipated in rent charges. Shares were £38,740 subscribed, leaving £16,260 outstanding.

The whole assets of the company, amounting to £36,740 were expended - £26,694 in land purchase and the rest in legal and engineering expenses. Despair was apparent when, for example, it was suggested that *"gentlemen of North and South Shields who frequent Rothbury and its neighbourhood are greatly interested in the completion of the railway - it is believed many would take up shares if the state of affairs was laid before them. However, 107 owners and occupiers in the Vale of Coquet had taken up shares. It is impossible to raise the whole money required in this district without the assistance of large landowners. This meeting pledges itself to co-operate with the directors in their endeavours to raise money".* It ended with a memorial to the Duke of Northumberland because of "the urgent need of His Grace's liberal support and pecuniary interest". Finally, it was indicated that shares were only £10 each and "that stalwart of Northumberland railways", Mr Tone, the engineer of the line and shortly to be dismissed, had agreed to take £1000 in shares". £1,400 was taken at the Rothbury meeting so that £2,400 of the £16,000 was already subscribed.

The Northumberland Central Railway Act 1867 (30 & 31 Vic-session 12th April 1867) authorised the N.C.R to abandon a portion of their authorised line, from a point in the parish of Rothbury 12 miles and 5 furlongs from the south end. It would not prejudice the rights of owners to receive compensation and the capital was reduced to £75,000.

As we are aware, 1866 hit the construction industry hard, and, as so often, the smaller businesses suffered. This was particularly so in the case of the N.C.R where the contractor, Mr Dowson, managing several smaller sub-contractors, was financially struggling. The effect on these can best be summed up in quoting one letter;

Winlaton,
Blaydon upon Tyne.
May 13 1867

To the Directors of the Central Northumberland Railway(sic).

Gentlemen,
We the inspectors of Messrs Lough and Wells Estate are anxious to get to work to complete contracts No 1,2 and 3 during the summer months, so as in the event of you not ordering us to do so, we shall commence forthwith and carry out the work with energy.
If the railway company are not in a position to make us monthly contract payments [an agreement] be come to, either to suspend the works for a term or terminate the contract now. We cannot afford to stay in this state of uncertainty,
Your most obedient servants,
George Nicholson, James Thomas King,
Inspectors of Messrs Lough and Wells.

To which was added an illuminating postscript:

"We attended at Morpeth yesterday for the purpose of receiving instruction....but were informed by the Secretary that no meeting would be held, there not being a quorum of directors".

The summer of 1867 saw fluctuating views as to how, if at all, to proceed. Progress on construction was by this time at a standstill, and the sub-contractors were restless with plant and men standing idle. Worst of all for the fortunes of the company, divisions appeared within The Board, though how far one can say there was a "Hodgson factor" as suggested by Jenkins is difficult to assess.

Certainly at The Board meeting on 11th June, the directors minuted that they regretted that they had entirely failed to raise the capital required. The directors were compelled to express their opinion that it is no longer possible to avoid abandoning the undertaking. The directors have ordered an extraordinary general meeting of the shareholders so that they may decide whether they will adopt this course. Mr Hodgson has already signified his desire to retire. The directors did not have the authority to express a similar wish on behalf of Sir Walter Trevelyan and Sir Horace St Paul. They remain firmly convinced that, if a comparatively small additional sum of money can be raised, the line from Scots Gap to Rothbury may be finished. The notice of the extraordinary general meeting proposing abandonment to be held at The White Swan, Alnwick on Saturday 29th June at 2 o'clock was issued by The Secretary from the Newgate St offices of the Northumberland Central Railway, Morpeth on 12th June 1867.

The Northern Daily Express of July 1st 1867 carried two features regarding the N.C.R. The first stated the obvious, that unless further capital was forthcoming all that already invested would be sacrificed. If they boldly expressed regrets that the Duke of Northumberland "should not see his way clearly to taking up any portion of the capital his willingness to grant a loan may be a point gained. [The Duke's £13,860 could never have been a loan] His Grace's present attitude must be regarded as his approval" (and then goes on at length to exhort all in the district to take up shares). The second article was with regard to the extraordinary general meeting "to consider the report of the directors recommending abandonment of the railway. The Chairman (and the newspaper) "trusted that there would be some way found to avoid such a calamity". Sir John Swinburne summarised the position with regard to buildings as "rails and sleepers laid - value £6,510 6s 4d (if sold might raise £4000). Liabilities including retention money £4,857 16s 10d, thus leaving a deficit of £800. Also claims might be laid on the shareholders for non-fulfillment of contracts. The Rev. Thomas Ilderton of Felton suggested that the directors remain in office. This was supported by

Mr Matthewson of Glanton. Both felt that the existing directors were best qualified to get them out of the current mess. Sir John Swinburne suggested that shareholders increase their number of shares by 25-30% to meet liabilities. Various small offers of share take-up were made in the light of the prospects of £13,860 coming from The Duke(8).

The August 1867 meeting at The White Swan, Alnwick began with a resolution proposed and seconded that The Directors make a further effort to raise £6,000 per mile. This was clearly wishful thinking. The meeting did, however, receive the announcement of the salvaging of the situation by The Duke of Northumberland taking up of shares as outlined above, but this was conditional upon the outstanding balance (£30-40,000) being raised by public subscription. The Company had then agreed that it would offer £10,000 worth of shares at 50% and £20,000 of debentures. Sir John Swinburne pointed out the futility of this as it would raise only £10,000 [see above Trevelyan correspondence for the reaction of a supporter]. An approach to the Public Works Loan Commissioners had been refused

Sir Walter Riddell thought that - "it should go forth that the £44,000 would now be provided by means of the very liberal subscription of the Duke of Northumberland. The latest estimate of Mr Tone was ample and liberal. Admittedly there was still the difficulty of locomotive engines and that sort of thing, but he believed they must hope for the best".

This speech indicates the depth of the confused and woolly thinking of speakers which included on this occasion, surprisingly, the stalwart Chairman, Earl Grey, who said:

"... that they were proceeding upon an estimate of £44,000 being required ....but he felt confident that Mr Tone's calculation would be fulfilled; and that the railway would be finished for £38,000 which would leave them £6000 to dispose of. But besides that, he did not believe that it was at all desirable that a company of that kind should have staff or servants and buy rollling stock of its own. He was persuaded that the proper course was to get the line worked by some of the existing companies and Mr Tone...had not the slightest doubt that they should, from one or other of the neighbouring companies obtain a proposal for the working of the line to their entire satisfaction."

This resolution was carried with only one dissent - Sir John Swinburne. Mr Tone indicated that the principal portion of the works of the line was completed. Expense would be considerable if the contractors were made to work over the winter. If need be, he would leave less important works (for consolidation etc) over to the next spring. Mr Ord quoted the Jedburgh Branch as being completed in 11 months, including two bridges and now yielding a large dividend. And on that happy note the meeting concluded!

A letter to Sir Walter Trevelyan from Earl Grey on July 2nd said *"...very glad to find there is a prospect of the unhappy Central Railway being completed after all. Mr Woodman, however, does not yet know what The Duke means to do* [author's italics.]

On 23rd July, Sir Walter Trevelyan wrote to Calverley Trevelyan: *"(he) will contribute his shares if arrangements made to complete the railway but he had not now the command of money which he had when in India and whatever I give will be taken from the very modest provision I shall leave my wife and children...relief to know that there will be no further call on me. (He then proceeded to complain at length that he had received no dividend on P & O and the Pennsylvania Railroad dividend had consisted of stocks issued on but one third of dividend"* [the depression was international and continuing].

On the 29th August Grey wrote to Trevelyan: *"My apologies for absence from the half-yearly meeting. I hope you succeeded in completing the arrangements that were contemplated and that you have got the money you wanted for the immediate resumption of work. It certainly is most desirable that the railway should be opened at the very earliest date that it may be possible......Mr Snowball [agent to The Duke of Northumberland] seems to have given you much needless trouble by insisting on conditions for the Duke's advances which might have been spared......"*

On 16th September, Snowball wrote to Trevelyan as follows; *"In reply to my letter to Sir Walter Riddell of 7th ult...(there is) no displacement or alteration of grounds upon which the late Duke dealt (which) compelled him to decline the request made to him. The statement that the borrowing powers could be used without the whole share capital of £75,000 being subscribed was a printed statement of a meeting at Rothbury on the 30th April, accompanying a petition to the late Duke of Northumberland I am unable to agree with you that if the Duke had subscribed the £13,860 there would have remained to be subscribed a comparatively small additional number of shares. On the contrary there would have remained upwards of £19,985 6s 2d to be subscribed by other parties. With reference to your statement that Mr Tone considers the line can be completed for £38,000 instead of £44,000, I beg to remind you that the latter sum was handed to me as the carefully revised estimate of Mr Tone which I might safely lay before the late Duke, and not [underlined] as was represented by Mr Culley at the meeting of the 2nd inst, after I had [underlined] suggested a great many alterations as to the construction of the line - I feel therefore that I cannot with any prudence assume the change of figures. If the £19,985 6s 2d be bona fide subscribed for, in the true spirit and intention of the Companies Act of Parliament by perfectly responsible persons; and if responsible persons will come forward and undertake to advance the cash authorised by the borrowing powers; and if His Grace's own engineer shall be of the opinion that the line can be completed for Mr Tone's estimate, then the Duke will subscribe the £13,860 as originally requested"*

In a circular letter Grey was able to write that with this latter figure at par and some other shares taken up at 65%, the unissued capital was reduced from £34,744 to £20,000, This rendered it necessary to lessen the discount further to 50%. In a similar letter of the same date, Woodman amended the last figure to £20,884 and stated that in offering these discounted shares to subscribers it is a condition that calls be not made thereon until funds to complete the line are available.

The moral for The Board and shareholders of the N.C.R with regard to hard businessmen like Snowball was less wishful thinking and more reading of the small print.

On October 23rd Grey wrote to Sir Walter Trevelyan concerning the recent directors' meeting at Morpeth *"...fair progress has been made in getting shareholders to agree to the proposal made for them to take up additional shares. There were a good many from whom no answer to the circular letter addressed to them have been received, and that you are one of them, probably from being abroad.*

*I write therefore to ask that you will be good enough to let Mr
Woodman know as soon as you can whether you agree to what has
been asked from you...additional shares at the proposed discount of
50% ..an excellent investment and earn a fair return on the original
shares the cost of which will otherwise be lost"*
[We already know Trevelyan's unfavourable views on this
matter from his letter written from Nettlecombe to Calverley, outlined
earlier] (9).

1868 saw the passing of The Regulation of Railways Act. This
affected the N.C.R in only one way, this being the requirement to
separate capital and revenue accounts. This arose directly from the
1866 situation, and, indeed, if it had been implemented earlier, might
have obviated the North British financial crisis and the downfall of
Hodgson. It might have come at an unfortunate time for the N.C.R
which, as we know, was still desperately seeking any new injection
of capital and might have obtained this from a new breed of investors
not too scrupulous about taking returns from capital sources at least
as part of their dividend.(10).

At the February 1868 meeting, all the directors submitted their
immediate resignation in a document signed by Earl Grey. Work
had halted, the coffers empty and the appeal to the Public Works
Loan Committee had again met with a re-buff. The above mentioned
take up of shares by the Duke of Northumberland was now fully
realised to have conditions attached requiring £30,000 to be raised
by public subscription. The company could only match this with
£10,000 at a 50% discount and £20,000 as debentures(11). The
company had been offered £20,000 at 5% for 18 months by The
National Provincial Bank. This was in fact the cause of the mass
resignation of directors because in letters sent out by Woodman, it
was clearly stated that The National Provincial Bank would have as
a condition of the loan that each director became individually
responsible for his proportion of the loan - and this the directors were
not prepared to do. He also gave the first indication of a new figure
to appear on the scene - Mr (later Sir) George Bruce - engineering
advisor to The Duke of Northumberland. His quoted assessment of
rate of earnings of the line was £8 per mile per week. Over the full
12 month period this would have produced £4992, which, after
deducting working expenses of £2496 gave a balance of £2496 (50%
deduction) amounting to an equivalent of 10% after allowing nearly

£500 for salaries and incidentals(12).

Mr Benjamin Woodman suggested the creation of 7% debentures for five years and this was approved as a first charge on revenue. Surprisingly, in view of the above, the Duke of Northumberland's money could be used before new shares were called. Again, we sense the scraping of the barrel for a desperate attempt to find a solution to the financial problems.

The Newcastle press carried a full report but this did not stimulate any interest, hardly surprisingly. On 29th February, a meeting held at The White Swan Alnwick was poorly attended. The Chairman was G.A Grey. An ad hoc committee was set up to try and raise the £20,000 needed.

This had the desired result. At the re-convened half-yearly meeting on 21st March, The Chairman stated that eleven investors had consented to meet the required figure, each raising £1,250. It was proposed that the Directors were asked to remain in office and Earl Grey, Sir Walter Trevelyan, and Sir Horace St Paul (who expressed great reluctance because his interests lay in the north of the county at Ewart Park) were persuaded. William Forster Esq and John Ord Esq were re-appointed. Thomas Arkle and Willliam Weightman were auditors. If there had been a "Hodgson factor" at this critical stage it made no appearance. Earl Grey reconsidered his position. He had had enough and his letter of resignation as chairman was received on March 25th

However, we have evidence that the bait of discounted stock had continuing results in that in July, Mr Orde of Nunnykirk was willing to take up £500 on debenture and £250 of discounted stock. This is an example of a modest investment by a previously uninterested party. And there were others.

The August meeting indicated that the present Duke, whom we have seen to be pro-railway and prepared to put up money, was to have existing works and plans checked by Mr George Bruce, his adviser on railway matters. This was to present complications as will appear. At this point the figures known to us are, to say the least, confusing. The amended Bruce estimate of remaining costs was £46,533. This compares with the amended Tone estimate, about which Snowball had complained in a letter set out earlier, of £38,000 although we know the original estimate to have been £44,000. No wonder Snowball was suspicious.[The actual figure came to £53,388 2s 8d.] This was published on 25th August, when, in addition to the above figures the assets were given as £41 11s 3d bank balance, and arrears of call on share capital £247 5s 7d. The money available from all sources was £1094. The balance to be received from the Duke was said to be £2565 0s 0d. Preference shares available for issue stood at £7447 16s 10d. The margins were tight but at least matters had improved. Construction could now re-start; Sir Walter Trevelyan stated that the situation with regard to capital was:-

Sum needed to complete	£44,250
Received from Duke	£13,860
Sales at discount, as above	£ 9,640
Debentures	£20,000
	£43,500

Shareholders continued to express doubts about the accountancy system and it was announced that Tone's plans and estimates were to be checked by Bruce, no doubt at the instigation of the advisors to The Duke of Northumberland. It is little wonder; all the above figures and many previous ones must be viewed with caution. For example, we have no real idea as to why the Duke's investment was the figure of £13,860. Sewell has the ingenious suggestion that Earl Grey had suggested the issue of £20,884 of ordinary stock at 50% discount and it would appear that this might have gone a long way to creating solvency again. From this figure might be deducted £6,140 being repayment from chancery deposits due after a proportion of the line was built. By 1868 this figure might have come to £6,140, in which case the Duke's figure would have brought the figure of money available exactly to £20,000. This ingenious suggestion has the ring of truth in it but of firm evidence we have none.

An encouraging circular was issued from Woodman at Stobhill, Morpeth on 18th November 1868 to intimate *"that the directors had negotiated the funds which were deficient from Messrs Lambton & Co's Bank on terms which appear most liberal, and by the liability of those gentlemen who offered to guarantee, the repayment is made as small as possible. The bankers cannot require repayment until the end of the three years. They take debentures for their advances which they cannot sell until the opening of the railway, or at the end of the three years, when there can scarcely be a doubt that they will be at par".*

How this negotiation was achieved is not known. There was no obvious connection between the railway and the Bank. Moore makes the suggestion that one of Lambton's Directors was a local property owner in Rothbury and the surrounding district. This becomes more likely because property was owned by one director, Mr.Fenwick, as far south as Longframlington. Moore suggests that Fenwick acted with "local patriotism". Far more likely, Fenwick would see the advantage of a through central route increasing the value of his property. This is speculative, and it may be significant that the Fenwicks were not prominent in the 1881 Central Northumberland Railway scheme.

The February 1869 meeting, with Sir W.C Trevelyan in the chair, received the cheering news that Mr Dowson had been instructed to start work and the remaining sub-contracts were let. The meeting was surprised, however, to hear that J.F Tone had at some stage been sacked and replaced by Mr Bruce. The exact significance of the move is nowhere stated and remains unclear. There seems little doubt that, as Moore says(13) a situation had arisen in which two engineers were at work but, at least for some time, no construction was taking place! We do not know what debate went on in this period. Clarification of duties only goes as far as a letter from Benjamin Woodman to Sir Walter Trevelyan stating that "some decision must be come to regarding engineers. I do not see how the business is to be resolved. One; of whom orders (Tone) work and gives certificates which the Board are bound to pay; whilst the other (Bruce) refuses his consent [in some instances], without which The Directors have undertaken no payment. Sewell's comment on this merely indicates in which camp Tone stood(14). After all it cannot be otherwise than the duty of Tone, rather than Bruce, to see that the contractors obligations were carried out satisfactorily.

J.F.Tone had, admittedly, been struggling under difficulties, even before the temporary halt in construction, due to the sudden decision to sub-contract to four separate businesses. In his half-yearly report, he complained that the contractors had not the experience of "great contractors" (such as Warings). He foresaw trouble through errors in routine civil engineering practice. He even took it upon himself to write to Messrs Waring asking that they reconsider relations with the company - hardly within the remit of his contract(15). Work had recommenced by January 1869 and a month later, J.F.Tone, the Northumberland born civil engineer, was dismissed(16). The view that Tone was dismissed by Snowball, The Duke's agent, cannot hold water because Tone was in contract with the N.C.R Board, and could only be dismissed by it. Joseph Snowball was a powerful figure, but represented The Duke as one shareholder, albeit a powerful one. Jenkins gives the view, though the sources remain obscure, that J.F.Tone was a "Hodgson-factor" man, and therefore tarnished with the "through route" image. Once Hodgson was gone, Tone's position was vulnerable(17). If a Hodgson-factor even existed at this time, it is hard to see it being very efffective without the man himself at the helm. It may be significant, however, that Tone was dismissed when Hodgson was abroad i.e. without protection. Sewell regards the Hodgson-factor as insignificant. He would rather refer back to the Border Counties and Plashetts colliery days, when Tone, on the death of Nicholson became engineer and the Duke was "held to ransom" over the lease of the mine. Memories would be long at Alnwick Castle and it might have been the case that words were said confidentially to the Board of the N.C.R to the effect that the Duke would bail the company out to the tune of £13,860 - provided the company got rid of Tone. The Northumberland Estate would not want to be involved with a man with whom they had had such unfortunate dealings in the not too distant past. Within the limits of knowledge available to us, we can only speculate.

The August 1869 meeting was held at The Central Hotel, Newcastle, perhaps in the hope of obtaining maximum publicity. The Chairman was able to announce that work was going on apace and that the contractors were promising an opening in the Spring of 1870. Proceedings were being pursued against Messrs Waring to recover company money connected with the underwriting but the legal advice was that they were not expected to succeed. A counter claim had been instigated by Messrs Waring but an injunction restraining them from proceedings for breach of contract had been successful. A new shareholder called Mason appeared on the scene (a Rothbury man but possibly with Caledonian Railway connections). Some of his points were very general e.g. that there had been bad management on the part of the directors, which, as we have seen, may well have been fair comment. For example it was hard for the directors to counter his financial astuteness, with the bald statement that up to July 1867, £12,477 had been frittered away on legal and administrative costs but only £27,447 on civil engineering works.

The precise financial situation was certainly confused. Jenkins quotes Bradshaw's Shareholders Manual which indicated the figures for the first half of 1869 as follows;

Capital expenditure to 30th June:
£52,585 (£9,689 in the last half year)
Estimated expenditure to 31st Dec: £26,100
Estimated expenditure to 31st July:1870: £8,400
To meet this further expenditure there was share and loan capital to the amount of £42,448, authorised or created, but not yet received(18).

The information appearing in such a reputable journal should be reliable, but, as is so often the case, the recorded data is only as good as the input. Many times at shareholders meetings the complaint was that the accounts were presented in an unsatisfactory or unclear manner. One example, the August 1868 meeting was outlined above. In the autumn of 1867 George Bruce's revised estimate of remaining costs was £46,533. In spite of the fact that he had increased the maximum gradient from 1:65 to 1:62 to reduce the cost of earthworks, this figure was in excess of Tone's. Expenditure to the end of 1867 was £42,779 (19). The total would amount to £98,302 i.e. nearly £14,000 in excess of the authorised capital. Non-paid up shares quoted at the August 1867 meeting came to £17,000. This did not cancel out the Duke of Northumberland's contribution (20). In reporting this 1869 special meeting, The Railway Times stated that the securing of the £20,000 mortgage over 3 years at 7% with Lambton's Bank meant that the £55,000 target was thereby met so that borrowing powers could be exercised. Sewell points out that in order for the Lambton Bank loan to be legally effected, the £55,000. must have been reached (21). This would allow the gross capital of £75,000, as authorised, to be met. This certainly passed without comment in The Railway Times, and is a good pointer to the financial mess appertaining at the time and the difficulties in making an assessment over a century later

However, on this occasion, the matter did not go un-noticed by the astute Mason, who on 25th Sept 1869 issued a notice to the shareholders as follows:

"A committee of shareholders should investigate the affairs of The Company. Notwithstanding the personal attack made on him by J.Forster the Younger of Burradon, and the fact that he was one of the parties recently released from his responsibilities, he proposed the amendment; that this meeting is of the opinion that the affairs of the company are not in a satisfactory condition, a quarter of the money expended having been for law and engineering charges, and the company are likely to be involved in [further] legal expenses. It is therefore desirable that a committee of five shareholders be appointed to make a searching enquiry into the past expenditure of the company and its general management."

Mason was clearly the sort of man who smells rats, but, in spite of this, we hear no more of the proposal. It must be assumed that it was rejected.

1.   The February 1870 meeting was again back at The White Swan, Alnwick. The news was good. Approximately ten miles of line had been completed. The directors were negotiating with the North British Company to work the line. The bad news was that Tone's predictions had been all too correct and added expense was required to repair the collapsed embankment at Forestburn Gate and elsewhere. The Fontburn viaduct was not completed and its approach earthworks were in trouble. On the advice of their solicitor, J.H Lloyd, an approach was made to The Board of Trade to raise money under the Railway Construction Facilities Act, the sum sought being £6,500 immediately and £10,000 in all. Additional expenses were for a turntable at Rothbury, now the terminus, and for the station at Ewesley, originally a private platform for the Orde family but later becoming public. It was resolved that several parties be repaid sums advanced, written by the allottment of new shares at par and of debentures or mortgage securities. The list included The Earl of Durham, Earl Grey, Sir W.C Trevelyan, H.M. Morton, John Ord, Willliam Forster, J Wheallans, George Bruce, C Orde and The Duke of Northumberland, the total sum being £6,500.

The working agreement with the N.B.R dates from 23rd March 1870. The main points were;

That the permanent way costs would be met by the N.C.R with the number of men employed to be agreed by the engineers of the two companies.

The locomotives were to be provided by the N.B.R, worked at £3 per day, to include wages of engine driver, fireman, and cleaner and fuel and water, stores and interest, depreciation and cost of repairs. The maximum mileage was 75 per day, and if above 78 the N.C.R was to be consulted. There would be no payment for Sunday services unless authorised by the N.C.R.

Carriages and brake vans to be supplied by the N.B.R at rent of 10% of the value to include interest, depreciation and cost of repairs.

The N.B.R would find the wagons under Railway Clearing House regulations.
The N.B.R to run three trains per day unless otherwise agreed.

Station staff were to be appointed by the N.B.R at cost met by the N.C.R (this to include guards.)

Stores to be supplied by the N.B.R at cost + 10% for distribution.

Scots Gap rent to include toll over the N.B.R land from junction to station at £50 p.a.

Traffic arising on the N.B.R and terminating on the N.C.R and vice versa at listed fares (e.g. 31-50 miles at 1s 6d.)

Receipts to be paid over to the N.B.R on a day-to-day basis with monthly balance for working expenses etc and half-yearly general adjustment.

The working of the line to be under a joint committee of three directors from each company.

Hodgson-Huntley protested in a letter to Trevelyan that the above was unfair. The charges for engines he felt were very high, it should be 9d instead of 11d per mile. He quoted the cost on the N.B.R's own lines of 81/4d per mile. If an engine cost £2000 and interest was at 5%, this would be £100 per mile, making it 71/4d. Even the 9d rate would be 2d per mile extra or £3200 per annum. He went on to list in detail how the carriage and waggon rates were equally unfair. Nothing seems to have been done in response to this letter by way of re-opening negotiations. Presumably there was a general feeling that the N.C.R was lucky to get its line worked at all.

The statutory inspection was carried out on 21st September 1870 by Lt Col. Hutchinson on behalf of The Board of Trade and is reported by Jenkins in full(22). It was surprisingly routine in content compared with many, but some points are worth noting. First, the line was not passed for operation, but, secondly, under the circumstances which have been described, it is amazing that so little was in fact wrong. We know from his report some further details of the line. Rail at 60 lb per yard was used. There was nothing surprising in this except to indicate that standard main-line rail was used (it could have been lighter for a minor branch). The fishplates, often a cause of trouble, only got a brief mention. The sleepers at 3ft centres were half round, presumably therefore split-log. This would be satisfactory for a branch line but probably not for a through-route if this was still being remotely contemplated. The steepest gradient was 1:60, so Bruce had again made some alterations presumably in the interests of further economy. (as this was previously been reported as 1:62, one wonders if the directors were informed of this). One culvert (only!) was thought to be unstable with the recommendation that slow speeds be observed at this point during the coming winter. At Scots Gap station, facing points were to be locked by the signals when proceeding from Morpeth to Scots Gap. Planking on two cast iron bridges was to be ballasted. There was one (one only!) bad rail joint and additional spiking was required at Brinkburn station.

We gain further insight into construction from details which emerged after the accident on 3rd July 1875 (see below). Bruce had been compelled to re-design parts of the civil engineering due to collapsing embankments over the lengthy construction period. One large embankment and culvert over the Delph Burn was at 1:60 either side of the culvert. At the inquiry into the accident, Jospeh Robinson, a retired railway engineer, now a farmer, stated that the whole line had been laid with flat bottom rail spiked to the sleepers and there were no chairs(23).

It took a week for Bruce's gangs to put these recommendations into effect and a letter from Bruce stating that the work was done, was accepted without resort to further inspection. Bruce was, according to Jenkins, not familiar with Board of Trade procedures before lines were sanctioned for opening, but this seems unlikely for a man of his experience. More likely he did not know how matters stood with the Board of Trade on a line with no rolling stock or locomotives, either railway owned or contracted. However, he must have had some sort of discussions with the inspector, for example with regard to axle weights. All in all it must have been a difficult situation for him, knowing that he was a replacement for Tone who still had his protagonists on The Board of Directors and amongst the shareholders. He probably erred on the side of caution. A train ran on 8th October(24). It is at this point that the directors sent the letter (one of the few claims to fame or rather infamy of the line), to The Board of Trade enquiring as to the meaning of "one-engine-in-steam" working. They should not have had to enquire about such an elementary point of railway working practice. It shows all too clearly their lack of basic knowledge and sums up more than anything else the amateurism of the enterprise.

The official opening day, October 31st, was the usual occasion of self-congratulatory speeches and much imbibing of toasts. Halloween seems an appropriate date to have chosen from the hindsight of history, because there were certainly ghosts to be laid!. The scene was The Rothbury Hotel - even if the official party did have to travel by a hired North British train which left Morpeth at 10.00 a.m. so that the progress of the dignitaries cannot be described as exactly rapid. Earl Percy M.P presided and the many toasts were faithfully recorded by The Newcastle Daily Journal of the next day. These included the Loyal Toast, The Prince and Princess of Wales and The Royal Family. The Bishop and Clergy of the Dioceses and Ministers of other denominations; The Army and Navy Volunteers; The Lord-Lieutenant and Magistrates of The County - and eventually got around to The Northumberland Central Railway, the health of The Chairman, Sir Walter Trevelyan (who was not present) and The Board of Directors. The reply was given by John Orde Esq, who specifically made appropriate mention of Earl Grey and The Duke of Northumberland, so that any differences and difficulties were now seemingly in the past. Significantly, Richard Hodgson did not get a mention, for, for all his faults, he had worked hard for the company in its early days. J.F.Tone was mentioned, even in his absence, as were George Bruce and the stalwart Benjamin Woodman. Other speeches were made by various civic and church dignitaries, of which the one made by The Rev.G.S Thompson, Vicar of Acklington is worth quoting because "he looked forward to the time when the railway would pass through Rothbury and onward to the sister kingdom of Scotland". Even at this late stage, and after all the trials and tribulations of the past years, the original concept of a central through route was not entirely forgotten.

The Newcastle Daily Journal gave some further statistics in a general description of the line. There were four stations at Scots Gap, Ewesley, Brinkburn and Rothbury (Rothley was a private platform for the Trevelyan Estate, becoming public only under North British ownership. when it was re-named Longwitton). The steepest gradient at 1:60 joined the sharpest curve at 121 chains. The heaviest cutting was at Thrum Mill approaching Rothbury, being 2800ft long and 88ft deep. The Fontburn embankment that had given so much trouble was 155ft long and the viaduct itself of 12 arches at a maximum height of 60ft. The summit was immediately to the north of Rothley at 694ft. The paper ended on the same theme as that of The Vicar of Acklington.(25)

The heady atmosphere of the opening ceremony did not last long and bickering between members of The Board and shareholders commenced. Those who had been supporters of J.F.Tone now blamed Bruce for many of the lines troubles. In retrospect this is hardly fair but out of it we begin to detect hard evidence of a 'Hodgson-factor'. Bruce had been engineering advisor to The Duke of Northumberland and a man of international experience, particularly in India and several European countries. It was from this background that he was appointed by The Board as replacement engineer, no doubt with thoughts of The Duke in the background. Hodgson and Snowball, The Duke's agent, were not on good terms and it may well be that this is how Hodgson came to support Tone. Jenkins reports at length the Hodgson-Huntley (as he now chose to style himself) attack on The Duke and his agent at the 1871 half-yearly meeting of shareholders. This was reported by the Newcastle Daily Chronicle; *"In most of his reports Mr Bruce has addressed himself to Mr*

Snowball, The Duke's agent, as though that gentleman had been The Board of Directors.... if Mr Tone had remained in the service of The Company up to the present time, the line would have been completed at an earlier date and at £10,000 less cost"(26). Hodgson had to write a grovelling public apology in the Railway Times, denying he had ever spoken in "disparaging terms" about their conduct.

We can perhaps read into this less of a substantial and co-ordinated attack and more the spontaneous and bitter utterances of a once formidable railway promoter, now a spent and probably sick old man. Bruce was well aware of the situation. He had been, and still was the servant of the Duke, in an advisory capacity, and replaced Tone for political reasons rather than on account of his expertise and civil engineering experience. Presumably the N.C.R directors thought that by so doing they would ingratiate themselves with The Duke, whose money was desperately needed. Snowball may well have had special instructions to observe and report back to Alnwick Castle on events. Bruce may have been in a position where he had to wear two hats and make two reports, acting in two capacities. If he was merely the servant of two masters, there would be nothing too sinister to be read into the matter.

Bruce, of course, easily defended himself in various ways. The most interesting point is that he denied that Tone ever suggested completing the line for £40,000. Here we are back to the poor accountancy practice and presentation of figures of the early years. As far as we know, the lowest total Tone ever quoted and recorded was £44,000. There were certainly justified additional expenses, legal, civil engineering, including the repair of poor earthworks built by a poorly skilled workforce and left for long periods half completed, and specific items such as the by now notorious Rothbury turntable. These figure alone would have brought the figure nearly to that of Bruce.. whatever anyone might quote of past figures it was the present ones that mattered and for long periods they had been desperate. Inevitably, The Directors had no choice but to approach the N.B.R once again and with that the next phase in events was about to open.

Chapter 7

The take over

It will come as no surprise that by this time the North British Railway was waiting in the wings. We cannot presume that there was actual collusion in promotion of the line, but from the facts presented, it is obvious that the leading lights were a fairly close knit group of Northumberland county gentry, to become one of whom Richard Hodgson had aspirations. We have also seen that the concept of the "Through-Central" route was not dead - indeed the 6th Duke of Northumberland appears to have made his investment conditional on this long-term objective. It is also clear that the Northumberland Central Board had made no effort to provide locomotives or rolling stock and were presuming upon the hiring of services from another company. There were only three local possibilities - The Blyth & Tyne, The North Eastern whose conservative management expressed no interest, and The North British still with Richard Hodgson at the helm. We cannot exclude entirely more distant companies, for which there were precedents (a classic example with a similar sort of history to the N.C.R, was The Invergarry & Fort Augustus Railway, worked by The Highland, whose rolling stock had to reach it by a tortuous route). In the case of the N.C.R, and with hindsight, we can say that there were no obvious candidates in the field.

Hodgson had been at the 1859 Morpeth meeting. He was a director of the Wansbeck Railway and The North British until 1866. There had been the possibility of a clear opening into Newcastle by co-operation with The Blyth & Tyne. This would never, as is often pointed out, have provided a reasonable route for passenger traffic, there being no chance of competing with the east or west coast main lines or the Waverley route. What it would have given Hodgson, and arguably the N.B.R, was bargaining powers vis a vis the North Eastern (and possibly the Caledonian) with regard to the all-important traffic rates. Favourable negotiations of these would have helped preserve his status with the restless North British shareholders. The N.B.R, having obtained access to Newcastle via the Border Counties and running powers from Hexham would become less interested in this route, and, as Sewell has pointed out(1), impeded the north-south traffic flow via Reedsmouth and Morpeth by altering the direction of the junction first at the former and subsequently at the latter. This in no way influenced the concept of a through-central route represented by projected lines from Scots Gap both north and south. The fact that the N.B.R did not inject capital at this time into the N.C.R (and beyond) was less a lack of interest and more the lack of cash. After 1866 Hodgson's dealings with the N.C.R, as he repeatedly insisted, were purely as an individual. This may well have been the case. Even though he was no longer a national force to be reckoned with, he had tasted power and liked it. Did he have ulterior motives of returning to railway development but on a lesser scale? As an ordinary shareholder, he had freedom of action available to him, and this might account for his ultimate resignation of directorship of the N.C.R.

We can only guess at his ulterior motives. They can best be seen in the light of a dominant and domineering character who had suddenly lost power. Born in 1812, by the age of sixty he was a relatively old man for his times, had driven himself physically and mentally hard as a captain in a very new industry, used every opportunity he could to climb the social scale, and probably by 1870 was already a sick man (though he did not die until 1877). His attacks on the N.C.R Board can be seen in two lights. First was the embittered old man exploiting what opportunities were left to him, in the full knowledge that those of the county set he chose to attack were never now going to accept him into their circle. His attack on and ultimate public apology to the Duke is evidence of this. Secondly, he had a vast experience of railway promotion behind him and it may be that he was viewing the possibilities of an expanded 'N.C.R.-complex' south and north of Scots Gap as either the largest possible promotion available to him in his reduced circumstances or even as a means of re-establishing himself into favour with the N.B.R by presenting them, handed on a plate, with a through main line from Newcastle, which, as we have seen was a long-standing N.B.R goal. Perhaps the best comment on what might have been going on in his mind was that he changed his name from Richard Hodgson to Richard Hodgson-Huntley. (Huntley was his mother's maiden name). It is almost as if the change of name was felt to be synonymous with an attempt to make a fresh start.

Even with a mere rump end of the proposed original railway to manage, the directors of the N.C.R continued to be plagued with financial problems. The 16th half-yearly meeting was held at Rothbury on 28th February 1871. The directors took pleasure in reporting that the line was open to the public from 19th October 1870. Negotiations had taken place with the N.B.R who had declined to work the line for a lesser period than ten years (possibly fifteen). The N.C.R directors resisted this and managed to hire rolling stock in an arrangement terminable in one year with three months notice. Bruce had reported that the earthworks were badly affected by the winter's severe weather. He was having to make up earthworks with ballast (not cheap) and the Forestburn embankment continued to subside slightly in spite of all efforts. Additional sidings at Rothbury were necessary. February 1871 saw £3,500 of the remaining £10,000 issued as preference stock with the same nominal 7% return as the debentures, so as not to discourage investment which might still come(2). This meeting at the Rothbury Hotel had to be postponed until April 3rd when matters were no better. At least the working arrangements of the line were now clear. The N.B.R proposal to work the line on a minimum ten year lease, was not felt to be acceptable. It did, however, demonstrate continuing North British interest. In ten years the recession should be over and North British finances improved - perhaps enough to begin further investment south of the Border. The N.C.R in fact hired stock from the N.B.R on an annual contract at three months notice by either side. £150 profit had been shown on the first months of operation (3).

A Board of Trade certificate of 3rd May 1871 showed that the company had raised only £71,906 14s 5p of the £75,000 authorised capital and could raise no more(4). Of the £7,500 of 7% preference shares offered only £1,625 worth had been sold. Mortgages and debentures amounted to £21,516 and rentals to £235. £9,600 was outstanding to meet the contractors(5). The financial state deteriorated alarmingly during the second half of 1871. By Feb 1872 the half yearly meeting showed a debt of £9,000 with little scope for further borrowing. It is not easy to see at this distance what had gone wrong. It may be that various factors were at work compounding each other.

The N.C.R total balance on 22nd March came to £10 14s 10d. On 18th April an amended statement of total cost of the line was issued. For what they are worth we shall record them, but they are far from satisfactory in that they do not make a coherent whole now as they did not to many shareholders then. All figures must be treated with reserve as ever with N.C.R accounting practice.

Total construction costs to October 1867 were £40,688 1s 2d. This had now reached £46,135 9s 3d. Liabilities at this date were listed as £8,247 4s 7d mainly due to:

calls in arrears	£1771 5s 10d
irrecoverable losses	£1524 0s 5d
shares owned by contractors	£800
balance of loan power	£1094
balance to be received	£2566
(from the Duke of Northumberland)	
balance from Board of Trade outstanding	£3500
(out of £10,000 additional capital)	
balance towards maintenance	£326 19s 10d

In a letter published in the Newcastle Chronicle on 23rd June, Hodgson-Huntley, writing from Carham Hall, gave his apology to The Duke of Northumberland and his agent in a letter mentioned earlier. In this same letter however he defended the figure of J.F Tone for the cost of the line as £44,258. as stated in correspondence at the time of the Duke's original subscription (£13,860). This may be of great significance in considering the figure quoted above.

The first and obvious cause was the overspending on most aspects of the line's construction from Scots Gap to Rothbury. This had come to a grand total of £54,383. J.F Tone had originally estimated a grand total of £44,000, rather more than for the Wansbeck Railway, but he had readily explained this to The Board. For reasons not now obvious, the Board had accepted the figure of £40,000 as the expected cost. George Bruce, Tone's successor, had constructed the line as far as Rothbury for actual costs of £54,383 on the balance sheet + liabilities of £8,247. His original estimate had been for a figure of £46,533. At the June 1871 meeting Bruce disputed the fact that *Tone had ever made a firm commitment* [author's italics] to the figure quoted (presumably the £44,000), but was himself under fire for a number of reasons including insufficient foundation work though there was a reduction in civil engineering expenses by increasing the ruling maximum gradient from 1:65 to 1:62. Moore suggests one feasible problem was the deliberate concealment of contractual obligations from shareholders. Sewell draws attention to the fact that Tone consistently underestimated figures and Bruce reduced the height of weather-affected embankments as the cheapest way of repairing this damage.(6) Bruce could explain some of these e.g. the provision of the turntable at Rothbury, not formerly intended to be the terminus of the line, but whether there were more is not known - for instance it is hard to see how he could have been persuaded to move Rothbury station nearer the centre of the town on the instigation of Joseph Snowball, The Duke of Northumberland's agent, without the full authority of The Board.

Whatever the case, the situation was gloomy, as the Newcastle Journal and Newcastle Daily Record continued to report. In August a new twist to events occurred when a sub-contractor of the company owed £870 took matters into his own hands by putting bailiffs into Ewesley Station with intent to sequestrate railway property. Messrs Warings were still pressing for payment not shown in a list of liabilities, and to crown all this, the trading accounts for the N.C.R for the half year ending 30th June 1871 were £,1707 revenue with working expenses of £1,597, leaving just £116 to meet all other liabilities.

Bruce was getting apprehensive. He reported to the Board on 8th August in the following terms; "He begged to state that the line and works of the railway have been well maintained during the past half year and now are in good order with the exception of the large culvert carrying the embankment over the Forest Burn, a position on the east end of which will require to be rebuilt.... this culvert was completely finished before I took charge... I lowered the embankment there nine feet because I feared the load proposed on it [was too great] and altered the gradient on each side". The total excess over estimates in my control [author's italics] is £2000 of which £1200 is at Rothbury station and connected therewith... it was stated at the last half yearly meeting that the late engineer of the company had effected savings of £3000 and that he would have effected a further saving of £10,000; it is extremely difficult for any man to calculate the amount of saving effected in work only partially completed.... the late engineer's estimates are in my possession from 3rd July 1867, when the estimate amounted to £44,725. My estimate and report to

Mr Snowball were dated 11th Nov 1867, so how that estimate could have any influence on one dated more than four months before, I am at a loss to imagine....at the time, I had not even had the honour of meeting the Board. The contracts into which the line was divided were let at £44,500...the total amount of money paid or due to the contractors was at the time of the stoppage some £22,781. The total amount of the late engineer's estimate to complete that portion of the work included in the contracts was with contingencies £24,000, making a total actual cost of completing the work £47,181 an actual excess of £2,681"(7). These highlights from a lengthy report give for the first time at least one man's comprehensive view of the figures.

There was no alternative facing the Board than to approach the N.B.R to negotiate amalgamation. Clearly, the position of the N.C.R Board was weak, whilst the N.B.R since the financial collapse of 1866 had greatly modified its predatory ambitions both towards existing lines and outlying territory. Some further figures will serve to show the hopelessness of the case(8);

Jan 1862 - Feb 1864; cash received to guarantee fund being the first call or balance of first call (including an anonymous donation of £1!)
£763 4s 0d

June 1867 (2nd 3rd 4th and 5th calls):   £11,814 11s 10d

1867 balance brought forward   £997 14s 0d

Nov 8th 1871   £5,473 4s 1d

Balance in hand on June 30th 1871   £25 5s 0d

Journal of N.C.R starting 15th Aug 1863;-
Sundries drawn on share capital account, first allotment of shares No 1-72
£48, 750 0s 0d.

share capital drawn to first call (£2 per share)   £9750
guarantee fund drawn to sundries 1-148, 149 etc.

£1229 18s 0d
calls in advance   £222 0s 0d.

The issue of negotiation was first raised by John Ord, one of the directors, at the meeting held in June 1871. He proposed that a committee of directors and shareholders should be set up to confer with neighbouring companies as to the working of the line. This procedure found little favour with those present, probably because, whilst most would be aware of the intentions behind such a proposal, few were prepared to face up to the issue. However matters moved quickly thereafter. Mature reflection prevailed and most of the directors would have as their paramount concern the saving of their estates. For the aristocracy, bankruptcy was a social disgrace, the sale of a railway proceeding through their estate of no shameful consequence, and one for which there had been many precedents. They could argue that they had served their estates well by causing a railway to be built and operated. Who carried out the operation was of little concern. Thomas Gow reported from Cambo on 10th October 1871 that terms were being negotiated. Waring's claim remained against the dividends guaranteed on the share capital but "as our London solicitors speak very confidently as to the final result, this need not disturb the proposed arrangements". Almost inevitably there was a compromise. Warings received payment of £1000 in full settlement of all claims and costs. A special meeting of directors was held at the Central Station, Newcastle, on 25th November 1871. It was resolved that the N.B.R be asked to insert the sum of £9,600 in the amalgamation agreement instead of the original £9000 agreed.

The N.B.R special meeting to finalise the matter was convened on 23rd February 1872 in Edinburgh. The N.C.R meeting followed the next day in Newcastle.(9).

These meetings were for legal and accountancy purposes. The effective date of merger was 1st.February. At the half yearly meeting at the Central Hotel, Newcastle on Saturday 25th February, the directors reported the borrowing powers to be exhausted, debts were £9000 exclusive of debentures. Unless means were found to meet this sum, the railway would have been managed by the Court of Chancery. Under these circumstances, the directors entered into arrangements, subject to the approval of shareholders, for the amalgamation. The basis of the terms were;-
1) Amalgamation date was to be 1st February 1872.
2) The North British to meet the expenditure of £9,600.
3) Debentures and preference stock to receive dividends at 3% p.a.

for the first five years, and thereafter at 4%.

4) Ordinary stock would have no dividend for 6 years but after that period to receive a dividend of 1% and after 1st.January 1879 to advance as dividends of N.B ordinary stock.

5) Various administrative arrangements were made, some merely transitional. For example, the monthly directors' meeting of 18th January 1872 received and approved a report from the secretary that the N.B.R was to draw the whole of the N.C.R receipts to 1st.February in consideration of its working and maintenance of the line, and at the monthly meeting on 22nd March, Woodman disclosed correspondence requesting the N.B.R.to pay a higher rate of interest for debentures, but the N.B.R declined this request.

The Northumberland Central Railway and North British Railway Amalgamation Act (35 & 36 Vic. Cap 123) received the royal assent on 18th July 1872. The feeling of the directors and shareholders of the N.C.R must have been one of intense relief. For the N.B.R the extent of the lack of importance is best summed up by the fact that the amalgamation always appeared well down the agenda of directors' meetings - indeed there are no records of this event to be found in the Finance and Traffic sub-committees records at all; but then the N.B.R had weightier matters for these sub-committees to discuss such as the proposed amalgamation with the old enemy, The Caledonian Railway. Thus at the meeting of directors on 14th October 1870, the N.C.R appears as item 13 (next to last), merely reading as "the manager submitted proposed agreements between the company and the N.C.R Co, which was approved", whilst at the meeting on August 10th we read as item 10; "The N.C.R Co proposed working agreement was read. The Board decline to consider the proposal that the Blyth & Tyne Co should work the Wansbeck Railway [and by implication the N.C.R] but repeat their offer of the 15 year agreement or of 10 years at 1d per mile for engines and wagons and traders rates and £100 p.a. for general management". [The precise relevance of this in relation to the N.C.R and the W.R is not clear].

On the 15th August, The Board merely approved item 10, the proposed agreement for working the N.C.R. Item 7 was the report of the committee appointed to meet with representatives of the N.C.R Co. The Board approved the reduction to 9d per mile for engine power in the arrangements entered into [reported as having been accepted by the N.C.R in minutes of the September meeting]. The October meeting merely approved the arrangements for the amalgamation as submitted by the secretary in a memoranda. The January 1872 meeting, as item 15 of 18 on the agenda, merely "noted the proposal that the dividend on the ordinary stock of the N.C.R should be anticipated by one year on condition that the N.B.R Co were guaranteed against any opposition to the Bill." C.J.Allen states without citing evidence that at this stage the North British Railway had intentions to extend the N.C.R northwards to Jedburgh. This would have of course been a logical alternative "through-route" development, if one accepts that at this stage this concept still held sway in the North British Board Room.(10)

On 25th July, Woodman amongst his last acts as secretary, wrote to Sir W.C.Trevelyan as follows:

My Dear Sir,
The Amalgamation Bill having received the royal assent, it only remains for this company to obtain the fund from which their liabilities are to be discharged. That this may be done, I shall thank you to sign the enclosed receipt, and thence forward, if by the first post to Sir Horace St Paul, to whom I shall write.
Truly, W.Woodman

And in reply, we have "a copy of the document sent to me by Sir Walter Trevelyan and signed by me , August 1st 1872 and forwarded by me on the same day to Mr William Woodman" (signed) H. St Paul. followed by;

Morpeth 1872.
Received by us from the North British Railway Co. the sum of nine thousand six hundred pounds, which we, the directors and secretary of the Northumberland Central Railway undertake shall be applied in discharging outstanding debts and liabilities incurred at and prior to the date of the amalgamation of that company with the North British Railway Co and their remaining due including arrears of rent charges, interest on debentures and arrears of dividend on preference shares of which the payment of nine thousand six hundred pounds the said North British Railway Company are hereby discharged.
(signed) Walter C Trevelyan

(signed) Horace St Paul

As Sewell says(11) "The Act gave effect to what must be one of the cheapest standard gauge railway acquisitions of all time". The North British paid £9,600 with which the N.C.R debts could be discharged. The legal battle with Messrs Waring was thus finally settled and Ewseley station returned to its rightful (even if changed) ownership. The terms for shareholders could have been much worse. On the debit side this confirmed the agreements at meetings on each side that the £21,516 in mortgages were to receive interest at 3% for five years after which they became 4% N.B.R. debenture stock. Ordinary shareholders were to receive no dividends for six years, then becoming holders of unguaranteed stock after a token 1% for one year. The £9,600 payment by the N.B.R bought them a line which at about £8,000 per mile building cost meant that the N.B.R paid about a tenth of the price of construction.

Let us leave the final paragraph of this chapter to D.W Moore(12);-

"The capital development of the Northumberland Central Railway Company provides in microcosm a picture of the immense struggle endured by small railway companies in the process and aftermath of 1866. By a remarkable mixture of ingenuity, illegality, and naivety the N.C.R directors steered the enterprise to survival. Divisions over alignment and interests within the county, mixed landowner reception, tenantry who could not be coerced, the 1866 financial crisis, disinterest of neighbouring railway companies, cash flow, cost and contractual difficulties were all handicaps that eventually were overcome" [to produce 13 miles of line].

Chapter 8

Parallel Events

After reading the previous chapter it may come as a surprise to the reader to find that the saga continues, and in more than one way. But, first we must consider events which had been taking place elsewhere in the county.

First, we must look at events occurring on the Blyth & Tyne Railway. This company, as mentioned earlier, tending to keep a low profile, gradually evolved from an amalgamation of colliery waggonways to which were added some short lines built under pressure from competitors. In general these proved successful. Thus, by 1860 it had taken a firm grip on the traffic of the South-East Northumberland Coalfield. In that year, possibly with prompting from the North British Railway, it decided to enter the Newcastle suburban scene because of the increasing population of what is now the south-east Northumberland commuter belt. An Act was passed on 28th June 1861 authorising several branches connecting South Gosforth, Shiremoor, Monkseaton, and Tynemouth to a new terminus at New Bridge St, Newcastle, and from Seghill to the Seaton Burn Waggonway.(1). B & T.R plans at this stage were certainly to carry as much coalfield traffic, both passenger and freight, as possible.

There were no obvious plans for expansion outside this area until November 1860 when plans were submitted for a line from South Gosforth via Coxlodge to Walbottle and Whorlton(2). Whether at this stage the company had further intentions is uncertain, but the reaction of the North Eastern Railway suggests that its directors got wind of something more than rumour. This would be compounded by the war of attrition beginning to build up between their railway and the B & T.R. Building under the latter's 1861 Act went on apace, so that the N.E.R using the lines of the already absorbed Newcastle & North Shields Railway was faced with a rival to North Shields and Tynemouth from a short distance away in New Bridge St, Newcastle. A further threat to North Eastern monopoly of traffic north of Newcastle came in 1872, when the B & T R Ashington and Newbiggin line was opened. Finances for the Blyth & Tyne were stretched however. Even as late as March 1874, when the country was slowly coming our of recession, the directors, at the half-yearly meeting, were forced to apply for an extension of time to complete the branch to Warkworth and Amble(2).

In the same year the B &T R sought and obtained authorisation of a new line to serve Whitley Bay and Tynemouth more conveniently. At this time, there was still the distinct possibility of North British access, albeit by this devious route, into Newcastle or south over a new Tyne Bridge. The N.E.R directors had had enough. They were strong and they struck. The Blyth & Tyne had always prospered and paid good dividends. The North Eastern had no option but to offer better terms, and this it did. The North Eastern guaranteed a dividend of 10% on ordinary stock, the preference shareholders continued with their bonuses as before and a sum of £50,000 was to be shared out amongst the stockholders(3). The Blyth and Tyne would have been foolish to oppose and the recommendation to shareholders was accepted.

So the North Eastern Board could well be expecting this to be the end of threats into their Newcastle territory, particularly in view of the financial collapse of 1866, which, as already indicated, happened to coincide with the deposing of Richard Hodgson from his position of Chairman of the North British.

If this was their judgement, they were wrong. The 1863 Northumberland Central Act had again laid the path open for an alternative through route to Scotland from Newcastle. The Blyth & Tyne's Walbottle branch received its Act of Parliament in June 1861. Using this as a launching point the South Northumberland Railway was surveyed, using our by now familiar figure of J.F.Tone as civil engineer. The plans were deposited in 1864 to be followed by the South Northumberland Railway Act (Vic 28-29 Cap 266) of 5th July 1865(4). Promotion of this line was by J.Hodgson-Hinde, half-brother of Richard Hodgson who also gave his support. The brothers between them had a wealth of experience in railway promotion as has been noted. Politically they were powerful and had many friends amongst the landed gentry of the area. But, in spite of this formidable partnership matters did not go right. Indeed, Moore(5) draws attention to the fact that no N.B.R money was forthcoming for this venture. The Act granted in 1865, still before the collapse of 1866, was for a branch line to end near Stamfordham, with very local directors, which apart from the above mentioned brothers consisted of the Rev.J.Bigge of Stamfordham, Sir Edward Blackett of Matfen Hall and Thomas James of Otterburn Tower. Of these three, only the last could have required an extension northwards to reach his estate. Clause 39 of the Act provided for The Blyth & Tyne to work the line but yet have no representation on the board(6). The conclusion must be that Richard Hodgson's sense of power had allowed him to negotiate privately with other persons and railways. He wanted that N.B.R direct entry into Newcastle at any price, perhaps, in view of his behaviour when Chairman of the North British, without too much thought for the legal niceties. There is some support for this view in the acceptance of the remarkable change of route of the South Northumberland Railway from that initially outlined. The original line proposed was circuitous and clearly aimed to have as much access to settlements in South Northumberland as possible. With that went financial support from the landowners, as with previous Northumberland ventures, including Throckley, Heddon-on-the-Wall, Ovingham, Belsay and Capheaton. Did Hodgson perceive in this venture the beginnings of a main line? Should a Stamfordham branch be constructed, then a more direct line could be the end result of a simple extension north via Kirkharle to Scots Gap - once again our "Crewe" of Northumberland? We shall never know what was in mind because neither line was completed. If the extension was planned, this differs from the view held by Warn(8) who with some justification argues that the whole matter was a blocking tactic in territory as yet not on the railway map. He points out that the Blyth & Tyne were forced to keep to their commitment in the case of the Tynemouth line, implying that the directors would not be bitten twice by offering a too concrete proposal. The matter remains inconclusive because of the buy-out of the B & T by the North Eastern Railway, the Board of which continued to promote the B &T Monkseaton -Tynemouth realignment as being a sound investment, but quietly dropped the north-western expansion to Stamfordham or any similar terminus.

Scant details are known about the S.N.R. We do know that the survey was of a line 23,286 yards in length at a cost of £44,500 12s 7d extending southwards from Scots Gap to Kenton Bankfoot. Estimates of land purchase were at £90 per acre. Engineering was estimated to cost £200 per mile and construction at £3000, which, together with the cost of permanent way came to £5,200, the total reaching £93,600. The Capheaton Lodge to Middleton branch with 200 chains at 1:67 gradient appears to have been in addition to the above. Indeed, it is stated that the Scots Gap, Middleton branch, Capheaton, Ponteland and thence north of Gosforth Park to the N.E.R at Killingworth was a route of 26 miles. This makes it look as if more than one alternative was considered at the south end, depending upon which major company favoured it most.(N.E.R; N.B.R; or B & T R)

Estimates of traffic were prepared. These indicated that traffic would total an estimated £6,100 0s 0d p.a., which with traffic from Rothbury and Coquetdale would increase to £10,767 0s 0d. The cost of construction was amended to £136,193 0s 0d. A dividend on £137,000 at 4% was deemed essential, which together with an estimated 50% of receipts for working expenses, gave a shortfall of £193 0s 0d. However, it was anticipated that the increased output of Throckley and Wallbottle collieries and Callerton coal to be worked over the line would produce an additional £3,206 0s 0d.

We must now go back to pre-1866 when rival railway promotions were still the order of the day. Thus the South Northumberland Railway as promoted, did not meet with everyone's approval because of the Blyth & Tyne (and by implication North British) connection. Subsequently, in 1874 Sir John Swinburne of Capheaton, a man with railway promotion at heart, had a line 23 miles long surveyed from Scotswood to Scots Gap(9). Much of the route envisaged followed that of the South Northumberland Railway with the exception of course of the southern end. This got as far as details of land ownership and possible associated expenses, but not of construction costs. The object of this exercise was presumably to involve the Board of the North Eastern. It had the support of the 5th Duke of Northumberland, with lands and mineral rights in much of the territory from Rothbury down to Newburn and Scotswood, who had already been approached by the N.C.R. It appears that he saw the advantages of a new through line from Newcastle to Scotland as linking his extensive estates in the west to outlets north and south. This is suggested in the British Parliamentary papers for 1882, when, in giving evidence on the Northumberland Central Railway, Sir Charles Trevelyan claimed that the Duke of Northumberland had pressed upon the N.C.R in 1866 "the expediency of opening up a complete communication from Cornhill to Newcastle," The Duke had "a valuable coal mine in the neighbourhood from which a great deal is expected" (which coal-mine was implied?)(10).

Proposed Railways in South Northumberland 1864 - 6

Berwick upon Tweed

Alnwick

Rothbury

Scots Gap

Kirkwhelpington

Morpeth

Kirkharle

B&TR

Seghill

Capheaton

Killingworth

Ponteland

Walbottle

Stamfordham

Dinnington

Heddon on
the Wall

Scotswood

Newcastle upon Tyne

Newburn

Carlisle

Northumberland Central Railway
- - - - - - - - - - -

Scotswood and Scotsgap Railway
-ı-ı-ı-ı-ı-ı-ı-ı-ı-ı-ı-ı-ı-ı-

South Northumberland Railway
-•-•-•-•-•-•-•-•-•-•-•-

Possible S.N.R extensions
+ + + + + + + +

Killingworth and Scots Gap Railway

One interesting point to emerge concerning the Scotswood and Scots Gap Railway was the interpretation put upon the Railway Companies Act of 1867 by Sir John Swinburne. This had changed the law relating to borrowing powers. Previously a railway could exercise borrowing powers once 2/3rds of the capital was fully paid up. In the new state of the law, one half of the capital had to be fully paid up and the whole of the bona fide share capital subscribed. Sir John argued that parliament rarely found fault with estimates being too high, so the best way to proceed was by making estimates higher than necessary, thereby gaining extra borrowing rights.

Whatever he had in mind we do not know, but he certainly had some homework carried out in detail. For example, we know that the total permanent way costs were given as £1220 2s 9d and the steepest incline was 1:67 at Middleton.

Swinburne listed the sources of income on the proposed route as follows:

1.   His Grace's Paper Mill, Lemington
2.   Falconnan Paper Mill
3.   Montague Colliery Co (R.Lamb, Axwell Park)
4.   Cuthbert Hunter Copperas Mill
5.   Carr & Sons Fire Brick & Tile Works
6.   Robson Common Brick & Tile Works
7.   Harrison & Co. Fire Brick Works
8.   (again) Richard Lamb Esq. W.Denton(?)
9.   Tyne Iron Works
10.   John Spencer & Sons
11.   Walbottle Colliery
12.   Throckley Colliery Brickworks
13.   Colbeck & Co., Manure Makers
14.   Reed Lampblack Makers
15.   Bells Close Fire Brick Works

Also in 1874, Sir Horace St Paul sought the support of the N.E.R in the promotion of a line from Killingworth on the North Eastern main line north of Newcastle via Ponteland to Scots Gap. This, perhaps least known of the various proposals 'on the go' about this time, may have had the greatest chance of success. In an interesting comment, Moore states "(that) the North Eastern, conscious that

Parliamentary notices had been issued for the S.N.R scheme, resolved that £100 be contributed towards survey expenses [of the Killingworth line] and indicated its willingness to provide the requisite rolling stock, should a railway be promoted. The N.E.R response is significant since its usual reaction to rural Northumberland schemes was negative. This suggests that the English company was prepared to fight the S.N.R and even the Scotswood and Scots Gap in spite of the latter's N.E.R -orientation, should a trunk route threat materialise. Was this yet another blocking tactic? If so, the conversion of the S.N.R to a Scots Gap connection from a Stamfordham branch terminus as outlined above, required immediate opposition whilst the original proposal did not. (though as argued above, this might have been ultimately necessary). Whatever the motives, and they were probably mixed, in 1865 there was the possibility of a route from Newcastle to Scots Gap which, in the end was never built whilst a scheme with real potential was put forward as late as 1874.

1866 was a watershed in British railway development. From 1863 onwards the ready availability of capital for investment diminished. Through 1864-5 the strains grew, financial confidence waned and banks and finance houses could only continue a limited service of loans to construction companies. The effect on the economy pervaded all walks of life including the landed gentry on whom the north and west Northumberland branch lines depended. In other times the S.N.R and the S & S G Railways, and even more likely the Killingworth and Scots Gap line, might have stood a chance of survival. Now there was none. We have not yet, however, reached the final chapter in our saga, but there will be a pause until an upturn in the economy.

Chapter 9

Northwards again

Of the original 45 miles of line authorised under the original 1863 Act of Parliament, we have seen how only 13 miles of line from Scots Gap to Rothbury were built, and a second Act of Parliament in 1867 allowed abandonment northwards. We have also noted in Chapter 6 how the legality of the all-important half-yearly meeting of shareholders in February 1867 was challenged, so that any subsequent actions of the directors could be called into question(1). Two points arise from this which merit consideration. First, by far the heaviest engineering works, including the Font viaduct were in the southern third of the proposed line. It was therefore disproportionately costly to build, as the evidence of the civil engineers cited earlier clearly demonstrates. Secondly, the distribution of shareholders is of interest. As Moore has shown, 92% of shares allocated were to persons with Northumberland addresses, thus demonstrating that it was very much of a "local" line(2). The N.C.R never had a" London faction" as was the case with say, the Border Counties Railway. The N.C.R directors were local gentry - one can certainly include Hodgson in this category whatever his other interest might have been. Furthermore 78% of local shareholders lived north of Rothbury(3). This locally invested capital would be placed for very local, indeed personal, reasons in contrast with, say, the speculative capital with which the country was awash during the period of the railway mania. The interest of those shareholders who were landowners in the northern two thirds of Northumberland would wane once abandonment north of Rothbury had taken place. Here lies the dilemma of such men as Trevelyan who appeared to have a dichotomy of view from the outset (see Chapter 3). We can conclude that the intention was to expect the North British or some other Company to work the line in one form or another possibly from the outset.

To start at the northern end would have presented easier civil engineering problems, and therefore cheaper construction costs. In an area of richer agricultural land better returns on capital could reasonably have been expected. - but this had one great snag. The northern end, unless substantial extensions were available towards Edinburgh would have connected with and therefore generated profit for the North Eastern. Why was this so unacceptable? From a landowners point of view, there seems little to gain or lose. The answer must lie in the contacts with the North British, in the case of Hodgson on a personal level, as compared with those with the North Eastern which were formal and so often sterile(4).

The 1870's were relatively quiet times on the railway front, in general terms nationally, and particularly in Northumberland. It took time for the economy to recover and, in the case of Northumberland, The North British was largely a spent force. In the late 1870's the need for better transport in the agricultural areas was again being felt. The financial situation meant that no serious attempt to resurrect the N.C.R in its 1863 form was possible at this stage.

However, others had shown a possible solution in the form of narrow gauge railways. These could be built at much less cost because the axle weights of locomotives and carriages and wagons were less, thus requiring lighter civil engineering and lighter weight rail. The radius of curves could be sharper and usually gradients more severe, which again reduced costs per mile. As they usually served rural areas of sparser population, railway architecture could be minimal. With this in mind 1880 saw a proposal floated to build the northern portion of the Northumberland Central connecting Rothbury and Kelso but as a 3-foot gauge line. This had support even in Alnwick, which still needed its agricultural connections with its hinterland. Sir John Swinburne was in favour, being a keen supporter of railway projections, but Sir Charles Trevelyan was less than impressed.

Parliament had passed an Act in 1846 stating that all passenger railways in The United Kingdom should be of 4' 8$^1/_2$" gauge and in Ireland 5' 3". (The Great Western, for example, had to abandon its Broad Gauge policy of 7' 0" gauge at enormous cost and disruption in order to comply). Parliament had, however, from time to time sanctioned railways, particularly in Ireland, of various gauges narrower than standard where it had been shown that the district required railway services but the anticipated traffic could not sustain the expense of promotion and maintenance of standard gauge lines. Generally, such lines were mere feeders to standard gauge routes, but amongst the exceptions there was a possibility potentially applicable to the central-route concept of North Northumberland. This was for mixed gauge tracks. These were relatively expensive to construct and maintain, requiring three lines of rail and complex pointwork. One other factor bearing on the North Northumberland situation is that where the narrow gauge joins the standard, trans-shipment becomes necessary, a labour-intensive practice which even in the early days of cheap labour was a cause for concern. Certainly no grounds for justification of this exercise, or the alternatives such as specially adapted trucks to carry the narrow gauge ones, would appear to have existed in Northumberland, where in the rural areas all lines were operating in parlous financial states.

This narrow-gauge proposal did have a 'London Factor' in the sense that the engineers Cornelius and George Lundie were London based, but they had Northumberland County connections with the Greys of Dilston, although not with any landowners in the immediate area of the proposed line. Jenkins(5) makes the point that the Lundies may have been engaged in nothing more that a bit of kite-flying. But The Lundies were not fly-by-nights and had much railway experience behind them, including the international scene where many gauges were in use. Cornelius Lundie M.Inst.C.E combined the roles of Engineer in Chief and General Manager of The Rhymney Railway in South Wales. Apart from an interest in colliery feeders to his railway, he is noted as a man who ran a railway in model fashion, something of a front-runner in railway terms and a man highly regarded in railway circles. George A Lundie M.Inst C.E gives his address as Cardiff and 1 Westminster Chambers, Victoria St, London. They were men of substance who put a well-presented and detailed case in their prospectus.

This was published in Cardiff on 1st July 1881, under the title of "Rothbury, Wooler and Kelso Railway". In the light of previous chapters it is worth consideration in a little detail as it presents the only full evaluation of anticipated costs, returns etc for the northern half of the county's central-route hypothesis. The preamble notes their interest in the reports of "meetings and public print" concerning railways in Central Northumberland and the Scottish Borders. It claims that one noteworthy feature of these had been the desire to obtain railway accommodation by the action of existing companies and not by private enterprise of individuals. It then reiterates in summary what we have already noted about the failure of railway schemes in the past. "At a meeting to consider the subject of railways for Northumberland and Roxburghshire, The Marquis of Tweeddale is reported to have said that there was no probability of railways being made if the capital required should exceed the sum of £5,000 per mile, with any prospect of a fair return on outlay"

The line of railway they proposed was as expected with some notable amendments i.e. from Rothbury via Thropton, Lorbottle, Whittingham, Glanton, Wooperton, Lilburn, Middleton, Wooler, Akeld, Kirknewton, Kilham, Pawston, Yetholm, Primside, Morebattle, Kalemouth and joining the N.B.R at Heiton siding at the south end of Roxburgh Bridge and probably traversing the existing N.B.R by means of mixed gauge track to Kelso station. The distance from Rothbury to Heiton was 47 miles and to Kelso station, 50 miles. Such a railway would serve a district of about 200,000 acres, of which nearly one-half was enclosed arable land, and the remainder upland pasture.

The above route is listed by Jenkins without comment(5), but is of some significance when compared with that of the N.C.R. The narrow gauge was able to offer a route of greater length, allowing for more curves and steeper gradients to be used. The effect was twofold. It meant easier access from villages but, more importantly, direct access to more estates from which the capital might be expected to come - Lorbottle and Snitter for example, in the south, and several additional ones close to The Border. Short but steeper banks allowed, for example, both Whittingham and Glanton to be served. The price paid for this was of course, lower speeds and lighter loads with trans-shipment problems particularly for mineral traffic.

The Traffic estimated is listed in detail of which a few examples will serve here. Passengers, parcels and general merchandise were estimated at £5,000; artificial foods, manures, salt, timber etc at £1,375; livestock at £2,250; wool at £150; Grain at £22,625; Coal at £4,375 and Lime at £8,750 making a grand total of £24,525. "Without counting on the many additional sources of revenue which a new railway invariably opens up for itself, it appears from the above figures that the income would be about £10 per mile per week which is lower than that of almost any railway in Great Britain, and we believe can be safely taken as a basis of calculation". The usually assumed working expenses of 50% of gross earnings was thought to be excessive and the traffic worked for considerably less. "£12,250 will be applicable to dividends "which sum capitalised at 5% will give £245,000 as the amount which may safely be expended on the railway".

The estimate of cost was £3,713 per mile including stations, passing loops, sidings, and telegraph apparatus, but exclusive of land, or at a cost of £4,000 including land. (Note how this compares with the costs of the N.C.R in the 1860's) This was broken down into earthworks (£29,604), 37 bridges, accommodation and level crossings, roadworks, non-public bridge, culverts, drains and gatekeeper's houses (totalling £25,953), permanent way including fences (£70,875 for 471/4 miles), sidings and passing places, rail on the N.B.R at Kelso and Rothbury, 17 stations, telegraph, engine shed and fitting shop, land at six acres to the mile at £45 per acre and parliamentary and contingency expenses totalling in all £188,027. Rolling stock was estimated at £32,190 to include locomotive engines, carriages and wagons of various sorts. The total capital for making and working the line was estimated at £220,117.

With a net revenue applicable to dividends of £12,250 the profits would be equal to over 5+% p.a. on the whole capital expended. Whether one accepts these figures or not is immaterial to the argument that a very detailed professional schedule was prepared which must surely have been more than kite-flying.

The paragraph on the estimated cost of land at £45 per acre makes interesting reading. "....and it is believed that all, or nearly all, [the landowners] will be willing to deal with the railway company on very liberal terms, in so far as their legal position will permit....parliament may be able to render some assistance to those properties which are held under legal difficulties of any kind (e.g. entailment, which was rife). In the copy in the S.R.O in the margin in an unknown hand there is a comment: "8 acres to the mile and £150 per acre in cash the more likely actual cost".

The statement that the local landowners would be "prepared to deal with the railway company on very liberal terms" has some ring of truth about it - we have seen above where the share capital for the N.C.R largely originated and it was the richer agricultural areas with newer agricultural methods that needed transport the most. Various assurances are given with regard to the excavations and embankments, gradients not steeper than 1:50, bridges and other works sufficiently substantial with appropriate strength of material and track-laying "such as to secure that locomotives of the greatest power that can be worked on a 3ft gauge line may be used, and may be run at speeds of 25 m.p.h." [the maximum under a light railway order].

The proposed line "would begin and end in the system of the N.B.R.Co, and although it might not suit that company to subscribe to the funds, we have good reason to think that they will look with favour upon the scheme, and will give all reasonable facilities for the interchange of passenger and goods traffic at Heiton and Rothbury". A lengthy reference followed concerning mixed gauges ending with a costing of trans-shipment at Heiton and Rothbury at no more than "2-3d per ton if smartly done".

The prospectus admitted that a break of gauge was undesirable but the amount of traffic, it suggested, would never warrant a standard gauge line, costing £10,000 per mile, which the N.E.R. would desire to own and work; nor even a lighter railway which perhaps might be made for £1000 per mile less than the latter. "The only circumstance that could render a 3ft railway insufficient would be the rise upon its tracks of a considerable "sea-sale colliery", of which "there is not the slightest chance."

So far no allusion had been made to the necessities of the southern part of Northumberland, and to a line of railway which certainly eventually will be made from Scots Gap, or perhaps from the neighbourhood of Angerton to Newcastle by way of Ponteland and Scotswood. For this district it is believed that a 3ft railway would NOT be suitable, and that being the case, the railway ought if possible, to be taken up by the N.B.R.Co, or, at all events, under their auspices, seeing as all the railways at Scots Gap belong to them, and they have power to run into Newcastle over the N.E.R's Newcastle and Carlisle line... if the power for the northern line were obtained (assisted by the N.B.R Co) then the Southern would immediately follow, and then a through communication would be established from Newcastle to Kelso, and to the whole Waverley line of the N.B.R.Co....assuredly used, notwithstanding the break of gauge, for traffic to and from all parts of the N.B.R' Co's Galashiels, Jedburgh and Kelso lines south of Edinburgh. Traffic in stone from the neighbourhood of Ingram, syenites and porphyries, is pointed out by Professor Lebour of Durham as being of particular importance for exploitation.

The pamphleteers were pro-N.B.R. This makes the implied meaning of the statement re. - Southern Northumberland largely meaningless, for here narrow gauge track would have been cheap and easy in connecting the estates, works and villages. Was there some more subtle ploy afoot? We can only speculate at this stage, as will again appear in the final chapter.

Alnwick, it was explained was not included in the present scheme, because it was thought that not too much should be attempted at once, and the through railway seemed the natural thing with which to commence. But it would be easy, the pamphlet stated, at any time in the future to form a branch from the neighbourhood of Whittingham.

On the financial front parliamentary estimates did not exceed £188,000 because costs of rolling stock were not usually exhibited in such estimates, yet it would be proper to raise shares of £220,000 and following the usual course, to raise by debenture loans a sum equal to one-third at least of the nominal share capital. The power to issue debentures would arise so soon as one-half of the share capital were subscribed for the works to be put in hand, half the amount of share capital only would be required to be paid up, and that by instalments spread over two or three years,

One comment arising from the above scheme is that the N.E.R "line from Rothbury and Alnwick to Cornhill could not be used as a through route". This is arguably incorrect as is postulated in Chapter 11. Jenkins points out that the pamphleteers were pro N.B.R(6). Indeed, the northern terminus is specifically sited at Kelso when it could have quite easily, and more cheaply, been at Cornhill. (In that case, a branch would have served the valleys of The Kale and Beaumont Waters, hardly different from the Whittingham-Alnwick branch mentioned by the pamphleteers).

One fact is certain, the narrow-gauge pamphleteers meant business in a way the N.C.R never did. It will be recalled that the latter never costed out rolling stock, the assumption being that they intended the N.B.R to work the line from the outset. Here the narrow gauge line quotes a total cost for civil engineering and a cost for mechanical engineering in the form of £32,190 for "locomotive engines, carriages and wagons of various sorts".(7)

This project has been outlined in some detail, not just because of its novelty but because it has in some quarters not been regarded as a serious proposal. It was made however, when there was something of a fashion for light railways. The authors of the scheme went to no little trouble and expense to make their case and present it in an attractive way. Nothing more is heard of the scheme largely because of interest in two rival standard gauge proposals made at the same time, as will appear in the next chapter.

A final small point is that this line is sometimes referred to as "The North Northumberland Railway" but this title appears to have no official or universally accepted status.

Chapter 10

The Final Phoenix

1881 also saw a more grandiose scheme promoted, confusingly named The Central Northumberland Railway. This was a standard gauge line intended to follow in part the old Northumberland Central Railway. The proposal was novel in one way. It attempted to overcome the chronic shortage of capital available for railway construction by building the line in six separate connecting sections, as it were six separate railways in their own right, the one following the other in progression northwards. The intention was to establish a new terminus in Newcastle. This site would have been in Percy Street at right angles to Barras Bridge, in what is now the property of Newcastle University. The present Newcastle Playhouse box office might be on the site of the proposed C.N.R booking office - give or take a metre or two.! This proposal not only overlapped in time the narrow gauge 'North Nothumberland Railway' previously described but also another scheme, the proposed Alnwick-Cornhill branch of the N.E.R. Both lines are shown on an undated map (? 1881) published by the North Eastern Railway(1).

The line was to pass in a 'covered way' through the Town Moor for about a mile (shades of the arguments about the Kent line to the Channel Tunnel a century later). At Kenton it followed what became the alignment of the later N.E.R Ponteland branch, pencilled in on the original plans as a 'possible Gosforth Branch'. This raises the question of what the later promoters had in mind for the final development of stage 1 to the North East and North West of the Newcastle conurbation, now beginning to be opened up. The C.N.R proposal, however, had its route from Ponteland via Ogle to join the Wansbeck line at - guess where? our old friend, the Crewe of Northumberland, otherwise known as Scots Gap - or rather a few chains east of the actual junction with the N.C.R, by now merely The Rothbury Branch of the N.B.R. Of passing note is that, whilst this was never built, the route was ultimately used as far as Ponteland by the N.E.R, taking advantage of the 1895 Light Railway Order Act which allowed lightly laid, slow speed branches to be built. This success encouraged the N.E.R to continue the line further as a Darras Hall branch built on the southern end of the Kirkheaton mineral line(2).

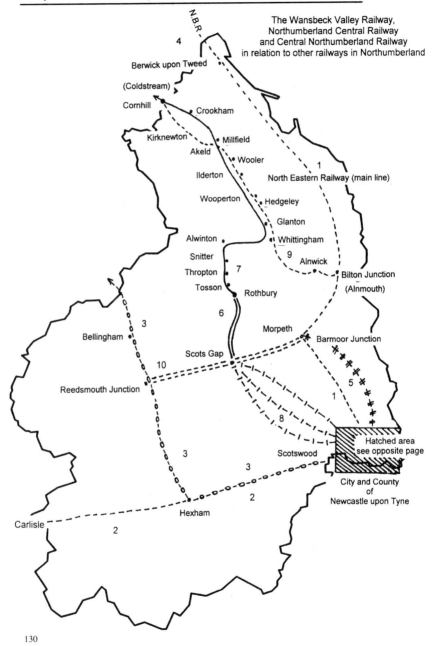

The Wansbeck Valley Railway,
Northumberland Central Railway
and Central Northumberland Railway
in relation to other railways in Northumberland

N.B.R.

4

Berwick upon Tweed

(Coldstream)

Cornhill

Crookham

Kirknewton

Millfield

Akeld

Wooler

Ilderton

1

North Eastern Railway (main line)

Wooperton

Hedgeley

Glanton

Alwinton

Whittingham

Snitter

9

Alnwick

Thropton

7

Tosson

Rothbury

Bilton Junction

(Alnmouth)

6

3

Morpeth

Bellingham

Barmoor Junction

Scots Gap

10

5

Reedsmouth Junction

1

8

Hatched area
see opposite page

3

Scotswood

City and County
of
Newcastle upon Tyne

3

2

Carlisle

Hexham

2

Newcastle Termini

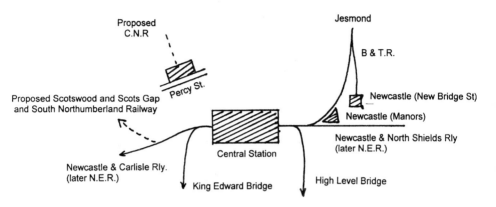

1   North Eastern Railway (East Coast main line)

2   Newcastle and Carlisle Railway (absorbed N.E.R.)

3   North British Railway. Border Counties Railway
     (with running powers into Newcastle)

4   North British Railway (East Coast main line)

5   Blyth and Tyne Railway (main passenger route only)

6   Northumberland Central railway
     (portion completed and absorbed by N.B.R.)

7   Northumberland Central railway (portion abandoned)

8   Central Northumberland Railway, South Nothumberland Railway
     Scotswood and Scots Gap Railway, Killingworth and
     Scots Gap Railway proposals.

9   Alnwick-Cornhill branch (N.E.R.)

10   Wansbeck Valley Railway

Railway 2, crossing the Wansbeck then by-passed the existing Scots Gap station to join the former N.C.R west of that station. Assuming successful negotiations with the N.B.R, this allowed 13 miles of route to be opened up in order to reach Rothbury. One wonders if, after a long period of North British stagnation, expansionary plans southward were once again to be placed on the agenda and that long-cherished goal of a terminus in Newcastle being attained? We have no evidence either way.

Railway 3 involved the duelling of the N.C.R line to Rothbury, with a by-pass around Rothbury station - for what reason one wonders? - Rothbury was by far the largest centre of habitation on the route. At first sight, it is hard to see why a company in the parlous financial state of having to build in supposedly self-financing sections would wish either to by-pass Rothbury or to build a second station there. There may have been some North British ploy here which is not documented and not now obvious. If this existed, it would have meant that the N.B.R saw the advantage of income from use by another company of its N.C.R line but drew back at allowing use of its Rothbury station. A more pertinent point is the difficulties in building a line immediately north of Rothbury. As Stephens points out there would be peculiar difficulties in preparing a route immediately north of Rothbury station within the financial constraints placed on the civil engineers(3). The existing station was situated at a low level a mere 60 feet above the river Coquet, conveniently situated for town traffic to cross the road bridge. Any direct extension from the existing Rothbury station would have interfered with this traffic, caused costly purchasing of property for demolition and bridging or at least a level crossing of the road. This line would then traverse the notorious flood plain between Rothbury and Thropton. If, however, a planned extension north left the Rothbury branch at, say, Wagtail Farm and progressed on a southerly curving alignment, south of Whitton, a station serving Rothbury would have been less conveniently situated for the town, but beyond there the line would have run along the lower slopes of Tosson Hill and Thropton reached with comparative ease. This would have had the advantage of serving the woollen industry at Tosson. Tosson is nowadays reduced to a farm and a ruined Peel tower, but was the site of a thriving woollen industry, possibly of great antiquity, giving employment to a local community and thought to be ready for expansion if better communications were provided(4).

Railway 4 continued the line from Rothbury via Tosson, Thropton, Netherton, Alnham, Glanton and Wooperton to Wooler. The Star Inn at Netherton is said to have been built as The Star Hotel in anticipation of the coming of the railway(5). This of course never happened but the substantial "pub" bears silent witness to local hopes.

Railway 5 was from Wooler to Sprouston (no details of this section are known to the writer).

Railway 6 was from Sprouston to Kelso. This has already been discussed earlier and requires no further comment.

A detailed survey, plans and prospectus are said to have been prepared and permission was sought to present a Bill to Parliament, but this was refused. The question to be raised was: Was this a serious attempt to promote The Central Northumberland Railway, or was it merely kite-flying in an attempt to rouse the directors of the North Eastern Railway into action to provide the badly needed rail services to the northern rich agricultural lands, and to the area west and north of Newcastle? If the first was the case, then it is surprising how poorly documented the scheme seems to have been; if the latter, then it had the desired effect both of causing Ponteland and Darras Hall to obtain railway services, and the Alnwick-Cornhill line to be built.

It is not intended here to describe in detail The Alnwick-Cornhill branch which is well-documented elsewhere(6) and often referred to as "The Wooler Line" this being the only town it served. We shall refer to it only where it is involved in completing the saga of the Northumberland Central Railway. The first point to make is that after years of disinterest, and perhaps as part of a shortlived and modest national second railway mania (though handled with much greater expertise than the first one), The North Eastern railway suddenly had a change of heart in 1881. This is perhaps not entirely unexpected because of the above mentioned C.N.R competitor and, indeed, for the beginnings of whisperings of other competition between Tyne and Forth e.g. The Manchester,Hawick and Glasgow Direct with London & North Western and Lancashire and Yorkshire Railway support of 1892, followed by Hawick support and initiative in 1894-1900. Also, one should mention the Swinburne promoted

Scotswood and Scots Gap extension to Otterburn, which might well eventually, have crossed The Border.

Perhaps the greatest threat of all lay in the Midland Railway (with a financial interest in the Forth Bridge). The Midland was ever, often with success, seeking expansion in every quarter. Its northern advance would have taken shape as the, nominally independent, Skipton and Kettlewell Railway (extension to Buckden) promoted in 44 & 45 Vic. Session 1881. Messrs Maddison & Co were financial agents, Raby and Wyatt Hoskins, parliamentary agents. Funded in the style of the C.N.R, its railway No 1 was of 9+ miles and Railway No 2 some 3 miles five furlongs in length to reach Buckden. Described as "The Midland Railway Extension Northwards" on the promotion map in the N.R.O, it had authorised capital of £120,000 of which £14,000 was subscribed and £5000 promised i.e. only £19,000 of the total required. The route up sparsely populated Upper Wharfedale can only have had northern connections in mind. In view of this, taken together with the details quoted earlier, it seems to have been rather more than a minor probing threat. Not surprisingly, in view of the finances quoted, it was abandoned in the same year.

The North Eastern reaction took the form of the Alnwick-Cornhill branch. Whether this was yet another blocking tactic which got out of control and had to be built, or was a well considered part of ongoing railway expansion, is, and will remain a matter of fine judgement.

Addyman has no doubts. He states: "The Alnwick-Cornhill Branch was built more for social than economic reasons. At the Parliamentary Select Committee enquiry prior to the Act being obtained, the N.E.R said that they were building the line out of a feeling of responsibility which was attached to a large and powerful railway company. With great care and caution they hoped the scheme might show a profit. They were wrong. The branch made a loss from the day it opened to the day it closed. Whittingham was the second largest station on the branch and earned about 16% of the branch receipts up to 1914. These averaged about £200 per annum(6).

The Central Northumberland Railway promotion would anger the citizens of Alnwick, whose railway lobby, going back to 1859 (see

Chapters 4 and 5) would doubtless retain their indignation at losing out on trade and travel in what they regarded as their hinterland. (Only the N.E.R Alnwick-Cornhill line served this purpose. The other 1880 proposals would have used Rothbury as a springboard for routes north.)(7). They were already at the end of one branch line and they didn't want to be, at best, at the end of another. They had support elsewhere in the Alnwick area from the Alnwick Board of Health, a body with wider powers than its name implies(8). This threat was very real. For example, at Glanton School on 4th October 1880, with Captain Carr-Ellison in the chair, the meeting proposed the route as predictably Rothbury-Whittingham-Glanton-Powburn-Wooler but with a branch line from Glanton via Shawdon and Bolton to Alnwick. The motion, proposed by Dr Robertson met with general approval of the meeting, but would have met with a frostier reception in Alnwick. This plan suffered a major setback when on 26th.March 1881 at a meeting held in Newcastle the anticipated revenue promised financial problems which would dog such schemes.

The N.E.R played matters coolly and, with good reason from the experiences they had observed, insisted that the support of landowners was essential. This was certainly available, for example from Sir Charles Trevelyan who inherited the estate of Wallington in 1879. He was a man of widespread administrative experience before his inheritance of the estate, was well known in Newcastle circles, and one of the new breed of landowners exhibiting estate management with a professionalism not previously seen becoming the norm. Wilson for example, assesses the Wallington estate in glowing terms "...."Sir Waltar (Trevelyan) too was one of the earliest pioneers of this commendable work (estate management) and as the estate is of considerable magnitude, he has more thoroughly and more persistently carried out his system of improvement than we generally find elsewhere". Sir Charles continued this progress by applying his own skills to the estate. He required better transport, was an N.E.R supporter (as opposed to the N.B.R) and publicly urged the N.E.R to promote branch lines and sought better rail communication to the north and west (of Newcastle) (9)

Wilson was the Professor of Agriculture at Edinburgh University and in "Notes of Northern Farms and Farming, published in 1864 noted, "The most acceptable supply of lime suitable for agriculture is on the Newcastle & Carlisle Railway near to Hexham;

but now the Wansbeck Valley Line is opened to Scots Gap, the new and extensive lime kilns of Sir Waltar Trevelyan at Elf Hill will soon be in a condition to furnish it at a considerable reduction on the present market price". He then cites estates needing lime cheaply and necessarily as being:-

Mr Matthew Bell of Woolsington
Mr Coplingwood of Dissington
Mr Ogle of Kirklees
Mr Riddell of Cheeseburn Grange
Sir C Monck Bt of Belsay
Sir E Blackett Bt of Matfen
  "[these] required better transport for their estates."(10).

We have, thus, all the makings of the classic situation in which the old guard struggles on to be ultimately defeated by the new brooms with their new methods. The latter did not convince the shrewd directors of the N.E.R of their case, however. They put upon them conditions with which it would be hard to comply regardless of status as will appear presently.

The "through-central" route concept was far from dead. For example, the Mayor of Newcastle wrote at this time to J.B Kerr Esq, banker of Kelso, saying;

"....the importance of establishing direct communication between the great producing districts of Roxburghshire and Central Northumberland and the consuming districts, of which Newcastle is the centre, cannot be overrated". (signed) J. Angus

Some took the concept further. J.B.Kerr received another letter from Dr.Patrick Kynoch of Greenlaw, dated 16th March 1881;

"...the present intention to carry the line from Kelso to Greenlaw, Westruther, Lauder etc; on leaving Lauder there are two courses which might be followed. First, from Lauder via Oxton village to Fountainhall station on the Waverley line. The second is to go instead from Oxton to the east through The Lammermuir range into East Lothian, joining the N.B. east coast railway somewhere about Tranent... by [the latter] you make a shorter line, intersect the best agricultural districts of East Lothian as well as travel through the *extensive coalfields of that county."* (11)

Thus in two letters can be summed up the new optimism, however misguided this might appear with hindsight. The concept of the central-route was in full flight. However, the opposition was equally vocal. Thus, in a speech at a meeting of landowners held at Alnwick on 4th February 1881, Mr Jacob Wilson said

"..the gentlemen of Alnwick and district had made up their minds that the time had come when something must be done to provide accommodation for Central and North Northumberland. There were easily surmounted engineering difficulties [and] having arrived at Wooler what advantage was there in continuing the line to Cornhill? It would simply provide a parallel to the existing [i.e. east-coast main] line and would bring no great amount of traffic either to Wooler or Alnwick. He would be exceedingly thankful, however, to have a line from Alnwick to Cornhill if there was no alternative route. But there were others e.g. Wooler, Vale of Glen, Kirknewton, Beaumont and towards Yetholm and round the hills to or near Kelso;...[or] by Pipton Loaning and joining the Berwick and Kelso near Carham, with the advantage of a further line north across the Tweed via Lauder to Edinburgh. This had been considered by other proprietors and Lord Tankerville is in favour. He conceived they would not be fulfilling their duties if they stopped there, for he considered the requirements of the agricultural trade of the district, Alnwick being only a part. He had had interviews in London with the Directors of the N.E.R Co and discussed the matter very carefully and earnestly and had had the opportunity to meet Mr Harrison (still in contract with the Board as a free-lance surveyor) They had both sincerely desired to know the feelings of the people of the district."

Much correspondence was engendered in The Kelso Chronicle on the choice of routes rather than the raising of cash. For example, J.B.Kerr on 24th February 1881 wrote in reply to a speech by J.Brunton at a public meeting in the Kelso Corn Exchange; "The rise and fall from Yetholm to Kelso is 263ft in 8 miles. This was in answer to the people who said that a Yetholm to Kelso line was a geographical delusion". D Sherriff of Lemit Law wrote; "there is no difficulty in making a line of railway from Yetholm to Kelso via Cherrytree, west of Graden, Ludenlaw and so to Melerdean(12).

In a letter to The Senior Magistrate of Kelso, J, Brunlees C.E, writing from Westminster on 8th.March stated;

"there can be no doubt that the railway on the north side of The Tweed would be a great convenience and a saving of time and money to the inhabitants of Kelso. Having seen the O.S map [there is] feasability of making a branch line having a fork towards Sprouston for the Berwick traffic and another towards Maxwellhaugh for the Edinburgh traffic. The former is favourable to be made but the latter would be expensive to make and costly to work on account of the steep gradients between Woden Mill and Maxwellhaugh station. I consider a bridge would cost £53,000 and a station suited to the town at least £15,000 more. Not knowing the price of land I think the branch would cost at least £75,000(13).

(Brunlees, a native of Kelso had extensive overseas engineering experience).

So far we have considered some of the northern reactions, this being so different from that of the 1860's when the Coldstream branch was abandoned through lack of enthusiasm and comment from Kelso was minimal. The southern element was still active, but as the following selection of correspondence shows, much more cautious. They had a right to be in view of their experience of two decades back.

We can start with a letter from Charles Inster to Sir John Swinburne of 7th January 1881.stating that there would be a meeting of land agents at the offices of Leadbetter, Harvey & Biggs, Newcastle to see if another line cannot be got from Newcastle to Scotland. "I have plans of the old N.C.R but we are at a loss, south of Scots Gap". Sir John replied on 7th February "about the meeting of landowners. Does this mean postponement of the January meeting, perhaps for lack of immediate support? If the meeting be well attended an influential deputation may be appointed to see the N.E.R directors and so bring about the same results as that you speak of in your letter, though not precisely in the same way". This was followed by a letter of 15th February to thank Sir John for providing maps of the portion south of Scots Gap." I shall get maps of the northern portion only, that is between Rothbury and Kelso. I am not sure that it will be wise to show a map to The Directors [of the N.E.R] .. if we go sufficiently towards Morebattle to satisfy the Duke of Roxburgh and Marquis of Tweeddale, we shall find we must go to Roxburgh not Kelso. It is clear the N.E.R Co will not go beyond their own system [Sprouston](14).

On the 13th of March Sir John was again writing to say he was "assured that the line to be well and truly laid would cost nearly a £million and is no light undertaking". On the next day he wrote to Joseph Laycock (Chairman of the B & T.R Co) referring to a meeting on 24th March with the directors of the N.E.R. He believed the best line was via Gosforth to Ponteland, Belsay, Harnham and Capheaton, west of Shaftoe Crags and thence to Scots Gap N.E.R [recte N.B.R], Rothbury, north of Trewhitt to Whittingham then to Wooler. Or the line might turn due north at Brinkburn and then via Framlington and Rimside to Wooler, using a natural gulley in Rimside running due north and south. (He stated) that The Duke of Northumberland promised support to develop Walbottle colliery. He continued about exhausted limestone stocks and how Trevelyan would benefit by opening his up. He set out the prospects for coal and concluded by saying that in his view the N.E.R was best to undertake this.

Laycock replied on 16th May, basically to express interest but enquire as to who would pay?

The views of Trevelyan and Lord Ravensworth appear below. Of the rest, we find most less than enthusiastic, an example being Francis Riddell of Cheeseburn Grange who, whilst not receiving Sir John's letter with great joy, kept the door open by inviting him "to come over and discuss it". Charles Riddell wrote, also on February 7th, to say that he had heard that, at an Alnwick meeting, The Duke supported the Alnwick-Cornhill route. R.J.Roddam had subscribed an initial £100 but when asked in November to raise this to £1000 said he was simply unable to do that "at the present time". Ogle had not supported the N.C.R in 1867 because "he was legally entailed and therefore but a tenant and cannot help". It is unlikely that the situation had changed much on that estate.(15)

However matters were proceeding slowly and in March, George Grey was writing a circular letter from Milfield concerning "Northumberland Agricultural Railways" (no "through-central route" concept here). His letter stated:

"it has been suggested that the promoters of these projected lines merit the thanks of the inhabitants of Central Northumberland for originating the scheme, in the absence of any other, and, also, that a fund be formed to reimburse them for any outlay. For this purpose an account had been opened at the Alnwick branch of the North Eastern Banking Co to the credit of which payments can be made direct, or through the branches at Wooler, Rothbury and at Newcastle"(16).

Great local interest was aroused at a series of public meetings. Charles Forster of Leadbitter Harvey & Briggs issued a notice of a meeting on February 12th " to consider the providing of increased railway accommodation for Central Northumberland and The South of Scotland by means of a line from Newcastle to Kelso, Alnwick, Yetholm (etc)". Sir John Swinburne described his experiences of fourteen years previously;

"The Duke has promised £60,000 and the rest must come locally, for no-one else including any company, will make it because the commercial advantage is not great enough. Any contractors would require ready money. There would be an advantage if the North Eastern Railway were to make it, but dividends would only be moderate. It would not be unreasonable to ask the North Eastern Company to mount up to the summit of the highest hills and dip down again to the lowest depths or make agricultural lines requiring tunnels. Alnwick people should be content to have a reasonable connection with the Wooler district by a line in the neighbourhood of Acklington to Rothbury or direct from Alnwick via Weldon Bridge".

Swinburne's thoughts were turning to a Light Railway(17).

At Rothbury a meeting in The Queen's Head Hotel on 31st January passed a resolution in favour of the line. The meeting pledged itself to write to The Duke of Northumberland and Lord Ravensworth and a deputation to wait on Sir William Armstrong. A Coquetdale Committee was formed. The Newcastle Journal reported the meeting in detail and from the list below, the remarkable fact is that the promoters of the line had changed from the 1863 landed gentry to tenant farmers and men of similar station in life. The Rev. Dr Auger was in the chair, proposed by The Rev.T.Ord of Shilmoor and seconded by Mr E. Carr of Harbottle. Amongst those present

PROPOSED RAILWAY EXTENSION

FROM

ALNWICK TO ROTHBURY.

SIR,

The Inhabitants of Alnwick in Public Meeting assembled some time ago, having appointed the Members of the Local Board of Health (with power to add to their number) a Committee to take every opportunity of increasing the Railway accommodation between Alnwick and the Western parts of the County, I have respectfully to inform you that you were elected a Member of Committee at a Meeting held in the Board Room, on the 24th day of November, 1870,—WM. DICKSON, Esq., in the Chair, and that the following Resolutions were at the same time unanimously adopted:—

1st. That WM. DICKSON, Esq., Chairman of the Local Board of Health, be Chairman of the General Committee.

2nd. That the Committee endeavour to effect Railway Communication with Rothbury and the Vale of the Coquet by a Line from Alnwick by way of Snipe House, Shieldykes, and along the flat ground towards Framlington, and on to Rothbury.

3rd. That Mr. T. THOMPSON, late Surveyor to the Board, having made Surveys and Sections on this Route as far as the Snook Bank, be requested to continue his services along with Mr. ELLIOT, the present Surveyor, to complete the Survey and Sections necessary to form a Line of Communication with Rothbury.

4th. That Mr. HEATLEY, the Secretary of the Committee, send a Copy of these Resolutions to each Member of Committee.

5th. That a Copy thereof be also transmitted to HIS GRACE THE DUKE OF NORTHUMBERLAND and to THE RIGHT HONOURABLE EARL GREY.

6th. That the Secretary summon, by Advertisement in the *Alnwick Mercury*, a Meeting of the General Committee when the Preliminary Survey is completed, or as soon as he may think necessary.

I am,

Your obedient Servant,

JAMES HEATLEY,

Secretary.

ALNWICK, 25th November, 1870.

141

were;-

Mr Donkin, Bywell; Dr Barrow, Rothbury; T.Hindmarsh, Elsdon; P Dodds, Biddlestone; J.Carr, Wagtail; R Handyside, Cambo; H.Scott, Alnham; Mr Lambton, Newcastle; R. Ashton, Tosson; A. Carr, Harbottle; W.Pringle, Branton; R.Donkin*, Rothbury; J.Whealans, Flotterton; J.Howey, Hepple; G. Turnbull, Glanton; H.Crisp, Prendwick; E. Hall, Trewitt; S. Langdale, Morpeth; W Forster, Burradon; J. Dodds, Peel; A.Drysdale, Elilaw; W Brown, Yetlington; G Drysdale, Great Ryle; Dr Richardson, Harbottle; (and a large Rothbury turnout).

*Donkin was the owner of the Rothbury Livestock Mart.

The Chairman's opening remarks included "....they had been kind enough to ask him to preside over the meetings on several occasions. Rothbury had been brought into communication with the rest of the world but the bit of railway they had got was a great disappointment. Rothbury was not a station on a line leading direct from London to Edinburgh but only stuck in a corner. They should show that they could pay for what they wanted".

Mr Whealans stated that the railway from Rothbury to Newcastle was tedious. He proposed the motion: That in the opinion of this meeting, it is most desirable that Central Northumberland should be provided with railway accommodation, and that this can only be efficiently done by a through line from Tyne to Tweed. Seconded: Mr Farrage, and carried nem. con. Mr Scott of Alnham proposed that the meeting pledged support to such a line and called upon landowners to use their influence to obtain a through line. "Between Tyne and Scots Gap are all kinds of minerals. The North is agriculturally rich ... they had no objection to a line from Alnwick to the North, but it would be much more sensible to have a throughline with a branch down at Powburn or Whittingham and then the communication would be complete". Mr Carr of Harbottle proposed;

"memorials to The Duke of Northumberland and Earl Ravensworth with copies to the principal landowners; that a deputation await upon Sir William Armstrong; that resolutions be sent to the Members of Parliament, the Borough of Newcastle and The Border Boroughs to ask their support. They must leave no stone unturned to get it; they must not let the Alnwick people or the people of the east side of the county turn them aside" In seconding this, Mr W Forster of Burradon said that "the North Eastern Railway had engaged for many years a monopoly of the county but he could not say it had done anything to deserve it. The North Eastern Railway had had a bitter lesson taught them lately. They neglected their duty in South Yorkshire and the promotion of the Hull & Barnsley line by another company was the consequence. The idea of the Midland Railway coming to Newcastle had been talked about, and he had it from a high official that if they waited upon them with a deputation influentially backed up, that they would not be able to resist the claims of the mineral traffic of The Tyne and Wear, and if they came to Newcastle then it would pay them to form a railway through Central Northumberland. The Alnwick people were now trying to get themselves a railway and he wished them every success. In Central Northumberland they were anxious that landowners, whilst approving the Alnwick railway, disapprove of a through line. In regard to Lord Ravensworth, he had large properties in the north, and was long connected with the south as one of its representatives. Lord Ravensworth must have warm feelings towards a constituency which no longer retained his able services in parliament. And again, as for Sir William Armstrong - no man had done more for the neighbourhood. With regard to mineral traffic, it was pointed out as one example that Mr Carr of Ingram is carting three loads of lime a week from Rothbury station each of two and a half tons and cattle and coal traffic would be off the roads to Newcastle." The meeting was reminded of the difficulties in obtaining coal at all during the last severe winter.

The committee formed consisted of The Rev. Dr Auger, D Whealans, W Forster Jnr, R Donkin, W Davy, P Dodds, W Hawthorn, G.F Drysdale, E Carr, David Dixon, R Farrage, T Allen, E Arkle, and The Rev. T Ord (with powers to add)

A significant point was that the Rev. Dr Augur had been in the chair "on several occasions", a memorial had already been seen, and that some sort of engineer's report had been compiled because "there were no engineering difficulties reported and no cuttings required nor anything that would make the line cost more than £5000 per mile". It was no use having a line for Glendale unless it benefited Glendale. (There appear to have been previous meetings and preliminary work done about which we know nothing.) The memorial may appear naive in the light of past experience, but the point of interest must be that it was made at all and by those of lesser rank than the N.C.R promoters of two decades back. The level of sophistication is remarkable in that, for example, railway services were felt to be the people's right and the level of debate enabled the example of The Hull & Barnsley Railway to be quoted. Also, behind emotionally charged feelings, there were people with two feet on the ground. Thus Mr Lambton of Newcastle said in his remarks "...[it is] better called The Northumberland Agricultural Railway".

Two letters appeared in The Newcastle Journal on the same day, both anonymous;
"Progress" hoped that the scheme would be a success if from Newcastle via Ponteland and promoted and supported by landowners".
"Rusticus" in referring to the Alnwick-Cornhill branch promotion, said that the N.E.R [would] retain its monopoly in the county at the least possible expense to itself. Artificial manures, feed stuffs etc were regularly carried up to 14 miles, a day's work, from a railway station. The advocates of the Central Line wish Alnwick to have the benefits of the proposed increased facilities by having, as pointed out in the memorial, a branch line from Whittingham"
The Newcastle Daily Journal of Saturday 19th February carried a report of a public meeting at the United Presbyterian Church, Morebattle, to consider the advisability of supporting the proposed railway. A large audience included Mr R H Eliot and The Hon. Mrs Eliot of Clifton Park, Mr C.J Cunningham of Muirhouses, Provost Young of Jedburgh etc. Mr Eliot was in the chair.

Mr C.J.Cunningham moved "that in the opinion of this meeting, further accommodation for the underdeveloped portions of Roxburghshire and Northumberland is urgently needed, and that this meeting views with the utmost satisfaction the resolution passed at Newcastle on the 12th inst. when it was unanimously decided that nothing short of a through route from Newcastle to Kelso, giving facilities to Rothbury, Alnwick, Wooler and the Beaumont and Kale Valleys will supply the accommodation required" (carried nem. con.).

Also at Kelso Corn Exchange a meeting expressed "the unanimous desire on the part of the County of Roxburghshire and the town of Kelso for direct communication with Newcastle and to urge the representative committee approached at Newcastle on Saturday last to push forward the projected railway". The platform party consisted of The Marquis of Tweeddale, Mr R.Eliot of Clifton Park, Major Wauchope of Niddrie Marischal, Sir G. Waldie-Griffith of Hendersyde Park, Mr E. Lockart, factor to The Duke of Roxburgh, Mr Smith, Chief Magistrate of Kelso, Mr.P.Stormonth Darling of Kelso etc. Apologies for absence were received from The Hon Arthur Eliot M.P Mr W. Forsyth, Merchant of Glasgow, Mr Snowball, agent to The Duke of Northumberland and J.Angus, Mayor of Newcastle.

In his speech, The Marquis of Tweeddale supported land improvement (in various ways) but thought that the cost of the railway would be double the £5,000 per mile quoted. He said "..[with regard to] the N.E.R and N.B.R, the N.E.R had a very strong inducement to strike a line through mid-Northumberland and the N.B.R had very good credit. The matter would have to be with appeals to the public and their landed proprietors."

On 22nd February a further meeting took place in Kelso Corn Exchange. It was proposed to consider a line through Mid-Northumberland to Kelso. Mr J. Smith. Chief Magistrate, was in the chair. Mr J Stormonth Darling stressed the need for a station in or near the town on the north side of the Tweed. The final motion read: "That this meeting gives hearty support to any scheme of railway extension which meets the requirements of the previous resolution" - all resolved and carried.

All this heady stuff did not convince the shrewd directors of the N.E.R of the case. They did not decline, which would not have improved their image, but they tightened the screw on conditions they required from the promoters. The Alnwick - Cornhill line depended upon landowners "agreeing not to exceed 25 years land purchase on reasonable terms"(18) .A Whittingham-Rothbury branch would only be considered provided that £50,000 was raised independently which with the general lack of interest or available capital seemed doomed from the outset, and a Scots Gap -Newcastle line required £100,000 similarly. As Moore says "in 1866-7 (i.e. in the era when there was still might be a fair amount of cash available for railway promotion) the Scotswood and Scots Gap railway could raise only £749. It is not suprising that only the Alnwick-Cornhill promotion was brought to a successful conclusion. For this the N.E.R may have had ulterior motives, as will be postulated in the Postscript.

Trevelyan was roused to anger with these requirements. He wrote:

"with your eminent engineers .... high credit which enables you to raise money at low rate of interest, you have.... the reasonable accommodation we ask. Half the expenses (of our railway) might have been raised from the bonus which you divided amongst your shareholders when you lately added £1.2 million to your capital"... *"under these circumstances, it is little better than mockery to throw back on an unorganised, miscellaneous, indefinite number of landowners and tenant farmers the responsibility of making a railway"*(19). Sir Charles Trevelyan was not writing to a company secretary. He addressed remarks to Sir Joseph Pease an acquaintance of substance and Vice-Chairman of the N.E.R

In spite of the gloomy outlook, the C.N.R pressed on. The memorial of the meeting on 31st January at Rothbury contained 1,457 signatures including 580 farmers, 442 tradesmen, 8 coalowners, 88 landowners (some of very modest means) and clergy, doctors, schoolmasters and hinds. The memorial was presented to the N.E.R at Newcastle Central station on 12th February. On 5th May Charles Forser, secretary of the C.N.R, issued a notice calling for £5 per share, thus, for example seeking £250 from Sir John Swinburne. In the meantime, independently, James Balfour Kerr, banker of Rutherford Square, Kelso approached the N.E.R Board with statistics with regard to Kelso trade for a population of 5,124. He gave details of the mart as "the largest in any provincial Scottish town", wool fair, agricultural show etc. The tup sales were the largest in the United Kingdom with sales all over the world. He had estimated that a line via Wooler, Mindrum and Kelso and thence to Lauder would shorten the distance between London and Edinburgh by 20 miles. His statistics for Morebattle (population 2096) even included the referral of patients by doctors for convalescence due to the good air. The route proposed by Mr Eliot of Clifton Park for the Wooler to Mindrum section would account for 23 miles of new N.E.R track. with running powers through 3 stations over 6+ miles of track. (The fact that this was the property of the N.B.R shareholders was ignored). This had the support of The Duke of Roxburgh and Mr Cunningham of Muirhouselaw.

The Star Inn, Netherton

A very detailed survey was undertaken by Mr Brunlees C.E and presented to the Senior Magistrate of Kelso. The attitude of The Duke of Roxburgh was crucial. He had succeeded his father in 1879. The Kelso Times discussed this; *"... it is held by many farmers, corn factors and other business people that the present attempt to procure a through route is a crisis in its [Kelso's] history. With a vast market and trains from Berwick, Newcastle and St Boswells, the town would revive [after the depression]. His Grace has decided to give every opposition to the new bridge and station. This is strange, considering His Grace promised all help to take a railway via The Kale Valley."* The paper quoted a letter from a gentleman, native of the town and well known in the chief continental cities, dated Edinburgh 12th March 1881:-

"I recollect well how sore a feeling diffused itself at the way the late Duke, or rather his advisers at the time, treated some 35 years ago, the projectors of the railway and the community of Kelso; and would fain have hopes, as I still hope, that his son might be ready, when the occasion offered, to compensate for this by congenial and kindly consideration. The Duke of Buccleugh had been able to manage with a railway both at Dalkeith and Langholm without reaping disadvantage from what has profited his poor neighbours. After all the fact is still to be encountered that to bring the railway to the town, and return it or continue it hence, must be far less simple a matter now than it would have been at first"

The C.N.R. petition to and deputation on the Chairman and Directors of the N.E.R. received a reply from York dated 9th May 1881. This was courteous and detailed and addressed both a through-route from Rothbury, a branch eastwards to Alnwick and the Newcastle to Scots Gap proposal. The directors could not see even a modest return on outlay. They would recommend to the shareholders the construction of a railway from Alnwick to Cornhill via Whittingham on condition that the landowners in the district engage to sell the land necessary for the line, stations and works at a price calculated on the present rentals and to subscribe or cause to be subscribed 2/7ths of the capital required, not a larger amount than £100,000 (already mentioned had been their terms for Whittingham-Rothbury at £50,000 and Scotswood to Scots Gap at £100,000). The directors' alternative is that the subscribers to any particular section of line should be entitled to an interest rate of 2%

per annum for 3 years and from that date 3% for the succeeding 4 years and then, at the end of seven years, the stock should be merged into the North Eastern Railway and become part of the North Eastern 4% preference bonds.

The directors must have known when preparing this schedule that the terms were beyond the means of local support. The largest promise of cash by far had been the £60,000 of The Duke of Northumberland. After that only the promise of Mr Carr-Ellison who had guaranteed £1000 was of any great size and at this time, no contributions had been received into the Guarantee Fund. Ultimately this latter crept up to £4,865. The C.N.R promoters met on the 17th May to consider the situation. For all Trevelyan's outburst, from this point onwards the C.N.R was on its own. A representative committee, meeting on 4th July decided to proceed with the Guarantee Fund of at least £5,000, to be formed to defray the preliminary expenses, on the understanding that it would be called up pro rata in such proportions as might be required. Sir Ralph Carr-Ellison and Sir Charles Trevelyan each submitted £1000 into this fund.

The first meeting of contributors was held on 3rd September at the Station Hotel, Newcastle, Sir C. Trevelyan in the chair. Present were The Hon. F Lambton M.P, Sir John Swinburne, The Rev. Eliot-Bates, Mr W.R Beck, Mr G. Burdon, Mr.E.Carr, Cptn Carr-Ellison, Mr R Donkin, Mr.W.Forster Junior, Mr.T.Gow, Mr.H.Middleton, Mr.F.Riddell, Mr.J.Robinson, Mr.J.Smith (chief clerk of Kelso) and Mr.J.Stevenson (representing Roddam estates). A circular letter recommended the appointment of a competent engineer on a fixed engagement to survey the line. The letter also began moves to obtain an Act in the ensuing session of parliament and the formation of an independent company to build the line. This could be either on a more limited plan from Tyne to Tweed or an enlarged scheme connecting the manufacturing districts of Yorkshire "in the direct manner" with Newcastle, Glasgow and Edinburgh (clearly this wider catchment area was aimed to obtain the injection of capital from other railway companies and individuals than had previously been the case).

Meanwhile, at Alnwick on the 15th September, a copy of a resolution passed by the directors of the North Eastern Railway was received. This read; *"that, subject to satisfactory arrangements being made with the landowners, with respect to the land which will be required, the directors will be prepared to sanction an application by the company to Parliament for a line of railway from Alnwick to Cornhill. It was resolved further that the terms of the foregoing resolution be communicated to the landowners on the route".*

The struggles and ultimate demise of the Central Northumberland Railway could be forecast. In an anonymous letter to The Northern Echo of 23rd December "facts and figures" wrote: "History repeats itself when the Northumberland Central Railway had to be abandoned north of Rothbury in 1867. Now the same persons wish to revitalise it. In 1867, Earl Grey offered shares at discount price, first at 75%, then at 50%. Even so, only £95,000 was raised and the line from Scots Gap cost £105,000 with sale to the North British Railway on condition they paid the debts. Those who put their money into the N.C.R prior to 1867 have received an average between 1/3rd and 1%."

On December 1st, notices to owners, lessees and occupiers of land were issued. These informed them of the application to parliament to be made in the next session for an Act, together with powers of deviation etc. These were displayed at suitable places such as churches and inns. The C.N.R company would have the following conditions:

Chairman - Sir Charles Trevelyan, Bart
12 Directors with a quorum consisting of 2.
The company offices at Armstrongs
Mr Forster Secretary
Mr Shelford to be engineer at £25 per mile excepting Ponteland-Scots Gap with a rate of £20.
Messrs Lambtons. Bankers
Cheques to be signed by two directors.

The directors were informed on 3rd January 3rd 1882 that the advance of deposit money by Messrs Lambton had been satisfactorily arranged and Mr Carr-Ellison, Mr W. Selby, and Mr.W.Forster had agreed to become security as an indispensable preliminary to getting an Act. Sir John Swinburne was asked but he must have refused, being a wiser man after 1867, because a second letter on 9th February asked him to reconsider his decision. He withdrew from direction of the C.N.R on 2nd March 1882.

However, the two rival bills were submitted to parliament in 1882 (45 & 46 Victoria Session 1882). The C.N.R Act allowed for a capital of £930,000 in 9300 shares of which 1/5th of the amount of shares was to be the greatest amount in any one call. The first share dividend was not to exceed 6%(!). Any mortgages were not to exceed £310,000 and the sum they might borrow not exceeding in the whole £75,500 in respect of each "£235,000 of the capital, but no part of the sum of £75,500 should be borrowed, until the whole of the £235,000 was issued and accepted. There were to be 12 directors whose qualifications were to be 25 (later amended to 50) shares. The promoters were given as Trevelyan, Swinburne, Ralph Carr-Ellison, W.C Selby, The Hon. Frederick Lambton, W E Langley, J Richardson, C.M Swarbrick and four others to be appointed.

On the 4th May The Directors made a call of five pounds per share. Then comes silence and no events are recorded until 1st February 1883 when a notice in The London Gazette gave notice of Chas. D Forster as liquidator of the Central Northumberland Railway Company with a notice of a meeting showing the manner in which the winding up of the said company had been conducted. The meeting was held at St Nicholas Chambers, Amen Corner, in the City and County of Newcastle upon Tyne on Saturday 10th February 1883. Cheques for the first and final dividend were issued on the previous day by Charles Forster as liquidator, Sir John Swinburne, for example, received a cheque for £31 15s 5d on 50 shares.

It is not hard to see why the North Eastern Bill received its Act whilst the Central Northumberland did not. On the Alnwick side, the 6th Duke of Northumberland had, through his agent Joseph Snowball, had a more favourable attitude towards railway development than his predecessors. Snowball, would have realised the almost impossible situation with regard to a through central route, whilst keeping an open mind on any one branch proposal. The Duke certainly backed railways, and apart from The Alnwick Faction there was support from Mr.Bryan Burrel, Mr.Rea of Middleton Hall, Major Browne of Doxford, Lord Ravensworth, Watson Askew, Thomas Ilderton, George Culley, George Skelly (for Alnwick Freemasons) and Lord Tankerville(20). He therefore backed Alnwick-Cornhill as being shorter, cheaper and fulfilling the Duke's (and Alnwick's) greatest requirements. This, and greater public awareness of the benefits of railway transport, may have influenced two Northumbrians, Sir Matthew Ridley and Henry Morton (manager of the Ford estates and a landowner in his own right) who had been appointed to the Board of the N.E.R. There was now what a century later would be called the "feel good factor" affecting railway development That Rothbury deserved to be on a direct route between Newcastle and Edinburgh, as quoted by the promoters of the C.N.R may with hindsight meet with surprise but it is best seen in the context of the above mentioned rival Carter Fell promotions. Trevelyan, a visionary, saw the possibilities of an alliance with that still most expansionary and competitive of all English railways, The Midland. The N.B.R however, had already learnt its lessons the hard way and took little part in this beyond making encouraging noises.(21)

Yet Trevelyan had his supporters, e.g. The 3rd Earl Grey, who wrote "respecting the proposed line from Newcastle to Kelso....I have no hesitation in saying that I think the construction of this railway would confer very great advantages..... the Alnwick-Cornhill would, I think, be of practically little use"(22) Surprisingly, some of the northern landowners favoured the Alnwick-Cornhill route, perhaps being influenced by the thoughts of North Eastern money being put into a scheme for the first time, perhaps thinking that this route would get them to London with only one or at most two changes of train. If from Whittingham there was to be a branch to Rothbury, one can understand Ravensworth support. As Moore states (23) "it is impossible to distinguish the financial, political or social motives". Defections from C.N.R support slowly built up, That of the Wooler area, still smarting from the burning of its fingers in The Northumberland Central affair in the late 1860's is understandable. Powerful figures like the Duke of Roxburgh petitioned against the C.N.R proposals and for the Alnwick-Cornhill(24). Most noteworthy was the defection of that doyen of railway promoters, Sir John Swinburne(25)

However, once again the North Eastern directors were on their mettle. If the original intentions were mere blocking tactics, they were soon swept along on a tide of solid support, as indicated above. To them, a branch from Alnwick to Cornhill presented the least problem which was certainly in a different class to the baling out of lame ducks as the North British had experienced on three sides of Scots Gap. Nevertheless, one still has the impression that the N.E.R was a reluctant hero in its victory over the proteges of the N.B.R. One point not mentioned in this situation was the fact that the N.B.R would get something out of the proposal. Having tried and been defeated on various tortuous entries into Newcastle, they were now presented with an alternative route to their Berwick main line, admittedly with greatly diminished financial reward but also nil capital investment. To the south lay the well-laid and proven N.E.R main line with access into Newcastle. If the N.B.R wanted to gain anything from this scheme it merely had to improve the network at the Kelso end. This would put an end to the threats which were growing, as already mentioned, from any Carter Fell schemes, which could so easily have forged links with the rival Caledonian as with themselves, and who knows how, in the worsening economic situation for railways, running powers and other links might have been forged?.

For the North Eastern Railway the accountants had probably done their homework well for we have interesting statistics from Miss M. Brown(26) of Whittingham. In 1919 this station, well placed to serve the Vale to which it gives its name, showed a gross total of 8,562 passengers bringing in receipts of only £1,573. This station could be expected to produce receipts second only to Wooler. For the Scots Gap-Rothbury line we have detailed receipts from N.B.R days but little from the brief time that it was in N.C.R ownership. Moore quotes the expenditure up to 30th June 1871 of £427 on locomotive and wagon hire (presumably this latter should read "rolling stock") and £137 on wages, presumably hired N.B.R staff (27) The trading accounts for the half year up to the same date were total receipts of £1,707, expenses as £1,597 leaving a profit of £116(28). Moore computes the figure of 93% of income absorbed by operating expenses. Perhaps a more telling figure is a yield in the first six months of 0.2% on capital investment raised over the years with so much effort and frustration.

Indeed we might get a suggestion of collusion even at this early stage. When the N.E.R proposal was accepted, it consisted of a reversal of direction from the terminus at Alnwick, a long hard climb up and over Alnwick Moor, thence down to the Aln valley via the Edlingham viaduct and tunnel. Whittingham station with its significantly different layout came next and then via Glanton, Hedgley, Wooperton and Ilderton to reach Wooler. From there the line did not go direct to the nearest point on the N.E.R (Cornhill, now called Coldstream) but followed the valleys of the Glen and Beaumont north west, finally swinging round to reach Cornhill via Mindrum. From Glanton to Wooler the route followed almost precisely that of the rival Central Northumberland Railway. From Wooler northwards the scheme took in many of the advantages of the route proposed by the narrow-gauge project. Can we read into the situation one of four totally contrasting alternatives? First, does this mean that the C.N.R scheme was a promotional gesture, something of a catalyst, to give an overt appearance of opposition when there was none? Secondly, was there a serious intention to complete the line as laid down in the Act with financial backing and future grand-scale developments having gained the backing of major railways such as The Midland or London and North Western Railways? Thirdly, does it mean that the fact that two lines were proposed part of each of which ran along the course of the other was mere coincidence, this arising out of, geography?

There is an interesting fourth possibility. We know, as quoted earlier, that the N.E.R Board looked upon the proposed Alnwick-Cornhill route as something of a social service to the community and regarded the financial situation both short and long term with gloom. For a short time, however, the concept of the "core railway" was in vogue.(indicated in the diagram). This took the form of a well-constructed branch line, connecting with a companies main line or lines. The finances of such were beyond the means of private individuals, estates or companies. The core railway could then be extended by means of lines which could be afforded locally. Thus mineral lines could be upgraded. Light railways could be constructed under The Act as could roadside tramways. Estates might have very light narrow-gauge connecting lines, these latter being probably not public. There are a few examples of all of these. They had the merit of being locally affordable, giving a service and increasing the traffic over the core-line, thus improving its profitability. There are various possibilities utilising the Alnwick-Cornhill as the core e.g. Whittingham to Rothbury, lines in the valleys of The Glen, Kale and Beaumont waters, and even northwards from Kelso and Coldstream. This vogue died almost as quickly as it started, for the need was not being felt until, say, the 1870's after the national recession, and by the end of the century the internal combustion engine was beginning to appear on the scene making for a flexibility of rural transport beyond the dreams of the promoters. Thus, we shall never know.

The Core Railway Concept
Some examples of 'might have beens'

ⅢⅢⅢⅢⅢⅢ	Mainline railways and branch to Terminus M[U.V.R. Ry Co / XYZ Ry Co]
————	Core railway branch of Main-Line railway
················	Locally built feeder lines
———— ········	Later mainline railway built connection to give running powers, through traffic M to K

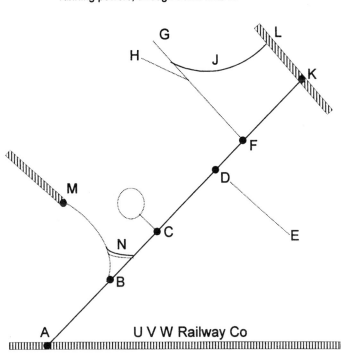

U V W Railway Co

A Main line railway junction station

B Village station at a suitable site for Light Railway Act "local line"

C Light (possibly narrow gauge line) to serve an estate. Not open to public

D Junction station for Tramway to isolated settlement (e.g a fishing village)

F Station for junction to Quarry (G) and additional line for passenger service to Quarry village.(H)

J Abandoned mineral line to Quarry, perhaps on a poorly - engineered route

K Junction station

L Abandoned Junction

M Branch Terminus (XYZ Railway Co)

N Spur, perhaps built by XYZ Rly Co, to allow through runners. K to M with running power

Chapter 11

Postscript

We have now reached the end of railway proposals and construction in terms of The Northumberland Central Railway and its appendages. But have we concluded associated matters which might have become railway history? The answer is probably not, and we are back to Chapter 1 and "The Broad Canvas".

We have seen that the Alnwick-Cornwall line was not, as built, intended to be a through route to anywhere It was a 'core' railway to which could be added local, in this case agricultural lines, now possible under light railway orders, lightly laid and relatively cheaply built and thus within the limits of local funding. [The concept of the core railway had a brief vogue, becoming obsolescent with the arrival of the internal combustion engine] This might include a Rothbury branch along the 1854-9 route, an Aln-Coquet line, and the revitalising of The Kelso, Morebattle and Yetholm proposal, to name but three. All these would account for some features of the chosen route. It was also suggested that one possibility was that the Wooler line was merely a routine blocking tactic , which, in the light of progressive public views on railway transport, proceeded beyond what was intended in a way which would not have happened a couple of decades back. If so, what was the best use of a doubtful asset that the very professional N.E.R Board and Officers could make of the situation? It must be viewed in the light of the whole railway scene which, after the 1866 depression and slow recovery, and before the internal combustion engine made serious inroads into branch-line profits. It was a time when branch railways were metamorphosing yet again.

The Alnwick-Cornhill branch was opened in 1887. After parliamentary select committees had been convened in 1881-2, the Railway and Canal Traffic Act had been passed in 1888. This arose from the unsatisfactory workings of The Railway Clearing House, first operating in 1845, when the railway scene was very different, and increasingly the cause of complaints, particularly in delays in payment. Rates fluctuated but were generally considered, inevitably, by the one side to be too high and the other to be too low. The Board of Trade had the unenviable job of attempting arbitration. At the same time there was a growing public awareness and distrust in monopolies. In the very heartland of the North Eastern Railway, the Mayor of Newcastle said *"(he) did but express the opinion of the trading classes of the North of England when he said that there was a great desire to have a railway competing with the North Eastern"*(1).

The above was said when Manchester inspired discussions were under way, yet again, for a new direct line between Newcastle and Glasgow. This surfaced in 1892 and it even brought that grand old man, the doyen of local railway promotion into the fray - Sir John Swinburne was not slow to see that the first part of the proposed route would pass through his estates at Capheaton, precisely as previous promotions as far back as 1867 would have done. By this time, however, he was a confirmed North Eastern man. Perhaps he had appreciated the financial implications in advance of construction!(2). Anyway, by the next year he was promoting an N.E.R Otterburn branch which might have been financially even more parlous than previous promotions. This would have had either the effect of blocking the Glasgow Direct route or being a catalyst to its future by injection of capital and take-over in the traditional style of the big companies. In 1894, a further Railway and Canal Traffic Act intended to clear some of the anomalies and frustrations from Railway Clearing House procedures, but seems to have had the reverse effect, for, by setting up a system of reports to the Railway and Canal Commission with the hope of operating a grievance procedure, it did not take into account the cost, thus discouraging approaches being made. The overall effect made railway companies keep profit margins artificially low with the result that railway promotions were no longer able to offer an attractive return on capital.

The management of the North Eastern Railway in the late 19th century had produced finance-related statistics which opened up the way to cost controls, far ahead of its time, certainly vis-à-vis most other railway systems. (It would take the depression of the 1930's to make the others attempt to catch up). It has been suggested, for example, that the withdrawal of passenger services on the Alnwick-Cornhill branch in the 1930's by the L.N.E.R (as successor to the North-Eastern, which was its principal and in terms of finance, only soundly based constituent) could be implemented so early only because the N.E.R had done the initial homework prior to the amalgamation of 1922. Indeed, by that date the reluctance to construct the branch in the first place, followed by accurate running and maintenance costing (by railway standards) may have already caused it to be pencilled in for closure. This could well have been but one example of North Eastern branches meeting a pre-Beeching fate(3).

We must now briefly backtrack to the days prior to the Alnwick-Cornhill branch being built. At that time, The Central Northumberland plan had been resurrected and The Bill accepted by parliament for scrutiny. It has already been noted that there were close similarities between the two schemes-the track alignment between Low Hedgely and Wooler is perhaps the best example, and that we can ascribe this to various factors such as chance arising from local geography and economic pressures but possible collusion, perhaps through the good offices of landowners such as Carr-Ellison, who seem to have had connections with both camps. We can accept the first without comment. The second is hardly likely in view of the ever-present and all-too-real financial constraints. We are left with the third, and this raises questions. We know that some of the great landowners were at least acquaintances of directors of the N.E.R and that Northumbrians had recently strengthened The Board. Collusion would certainly not have been difficult. The one side would have had its financial problems resolved by exploiting N.E.R capital. For the other it would have allowed easing the pressures of railway politics placed upon it, and, when the line ultimately was a failure financially, it could have quoted its senior officers as saying in effect "we told you so". A better public image would have been preserved, even although the much-criticised monopoly situation would not have been affected.

But had the N.E.R more grandiose plans for the Alnwick-Cornhill line? This will probably never be known for certain, but there are one or two pointers which suggest intriguing possibilities. If one accepts that the building of the line had probably been forced upon the directors by socio-political pressures, against professional advice, decisions would become necessary as to what best to make of the situation, and a common business gambit is to attempt to buy yourself out of trouble by further investment. Obviously, the usual financial risk factors applying to any business venture apply to a rural railway, and perhaps strongly. Bear in mind that over the years the North Eastern and North British Railways had been forced to work together

Lime Kiln

as partners in the East Coast route. They were never easy bedfellows, though the disharmony was arguably less acrimonious than that between them and the southern partner in the trunk route linking the capitals, The Great Northern, but bad enough. Suppose that a scheme could be devised which would reduce the North Eastern dependence upon an unsatisfactory partner North of The Border. There was precedent for this in the link that had been forged between The Midland and North British through the Settle & Carlisle and Waverly Routes. This had allowed these companies to develop through traffic without recourse to co-operation with the great West Coast lines, The London & North Western and The Caledonian, who, on the whole were staunch allies. This is harking back to the concept of The Central Route giving increased revenue from loss of mileage over 'foreign' track. We also know how the N.E.R Board had repeatedly outmanoeuvred that of the N.B.R in the past.

Thoughts along these lines might have been stimulated by the fright which the N.E.R Board got when the renewed Carter Fell scheme, with London & North Western backing surfaced. Was the N.E.R tempted to take bold action, and, for once, something more than blocking tactics? Look at the lavish buildings erected on the Wooler line as compared with those on other branches. Edlingham, Wooperton and Kirknewton or any of the other wayside stations were lavishly built with beautiful masonry. Whittingham is a special case. Apart from the site which is large and designed for a Vale of Whittingham cattle mart, the site of which is now used by Northumberland County Council Highways(4), it has besides a substantial station master's house, a line of employees cottages, carriage landing, cattle dock, large goods shed, coal drops, lime cells and two water tanks, suggesting freight traffic usage. The station is unique in that it is clearly made with the purposes of a branch in mind, and space for expansion of handling facilities. Was there an intention to build a Rothbury branch after all? (In fact two "branches" of a sort were built, one to tile kilns to the east and the other a First World War light railway for Canadian loggers working in the area(5)). But, regardless of possible branches, extend the platforms (easily achieved) provide goods loops and perhaps a parcels dock etc and you have a substantial main line station with full facilities.

Let us turn next to the Alnmouth - Alnwick branch and you will find that this was built to what the L.N.E.R later called R.A 9 standards.

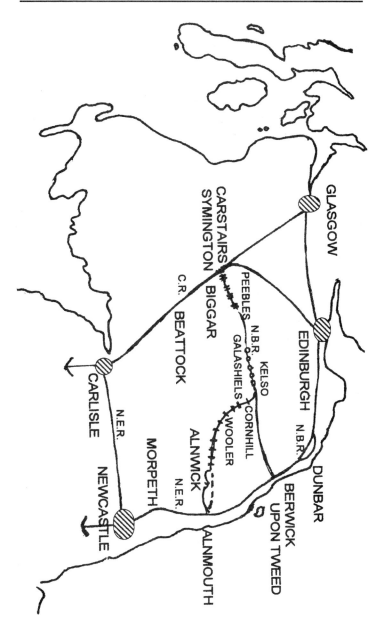

The Possible North-Eastern / Caledonian Railways "Cut-Off"
for London and stations North to Alnwick Traffic to Glasgow

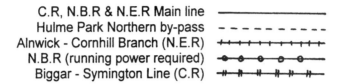

C.R, N.B.R & N.E.R Main line
Hulme Park Northern by-pass
Alnwick - Cornhill Branch (N.E.R)
N.B.R (running power required)
Biggar - Symington Line (C.R)

Traffic from the South on leaving Newcastle would have a
shorter route to Glasgow, easier gradients, particularly
eliminating Beatock, giving more economical working, and the
North British Railway, always a difficult partner in the East-
Coast and arch rival of the Caledonian Railway, would be
largely by-passed. This scheme would in many ways follow
the proposes Caledonian Extension Railway. It would also be
a route in the "through - central" conception and anticipate
late 20th century heavy road traffic which uses the M1, A1,
A66 and M74 to reach Glasgow and increasingly the A1, A697
and A68 from Newcastle to Edinburgh.

[R.A stands for route availability, and the number indicates the weight (and so the power) of the locomotives which could operate over that line. All L.N.E.R routes were so coded the range being between 1 and 9]. Thus it was built to take the heaviest and most powerful locomotives owned by the N.E.R and, because of good engineering foresight, of its successor, the L.N.E.R. In fact it could take most of the more powerful and heavy locomotives ever to run in Britain (the few exceptions being due to loading gauge and not weight restrictions). Was all that work done just to satisfy the disgruntled traders of Alnwick, or to allow The Duke of Northumberland to arrive behind, say, 'Flying Scotsman', or later one of those graceful A4 streamlined pacifics?

The usual answer is that such lines were built to this sort of standard to accommodate locomotives 'running in' after heavy repairs, or as filling-in trips between heavier main-line duties, a widespread practice devised in order to minimise locomotive-idle time. Both could apply to the Alnmouth-Alnwick line, being nicely situated at a reasonable distance from Newcastle's Heaton shed and from Gateshead where heavy repair facilities were available. But this could hardly apply to the Alnwick-Cornhill branch which we find built to the same standard R.A 9.(6). Indeed the Newcastle Journal stated "..all the bridges on the line were said to have been constructed to admit the doubling of the line whenever such shall be found necessary. The total cost of the branch was £500,000. The only obvious explanation of the justification of this outlay was that it could be used in emergency situations, as, for example during the second world war, or when the main-line south from Edinburgh was blocked for any reason.

So was there something more in mind? We find that, apart from one or two bridges in the Wooler area which would require strengthening, regular use could be made by large locomotives and doubling of the track provided for. It would have been possible for the world steam record-holder, Mallard, to pull into Whittingham station - not at the world record speed of 126 m.p.h. of course! There would have been no prizes for speed for any locomotive toiling up the long slog from Alnwick to Summit Cottages (with some of the gradient at 1:50) and down the other side with squealing brakes hard on for the restriction over the curve of Edlingham viaduct.

Chapter 11 - Postscript

It is possible that, in the changed circumstances of the late 19th century, public opinion and the known pro-railway views of the then Duke of Northumberland might have achieved a line through The Parks, north-west of Alnwick, alongside the course of the River Aln. Even if not, The Parks had been reduced in size to the east by a new alignment of the surrounding wall. This was to allow easier road transport to Eglingham without the need for gates and gatehouses with their attendant gate-keepers. This, in turn, would have allowed for a new railway diversion to the east of Alnwick, traversing the west side of the Heffer Law ridge to join the existing line at, say, Wooperton. The Parks would not have had their beauty and privacy interrupted. In fact very little of architectural grandeur or landscape vistas would have been disturbed. With the Alnwick slog a thing of the past, the way was open for a high speed line on gentle curves and gradients through Glendale and Tillside, diverting the east coast main line into the Tweed valley, via Kelso (with a neat bit of table-turning on the N.B.R) and on a gentle climb up the Tweed valley and into Clydesdale with, at most, a short tunnel at the Biggar Gap, an easy route used by all forms of land transport from prehistoric times. This would have led into the welcoming arms of The Caledonian - that arch enemy of the North British. The precedent for this we have already discussed, in, for example, the Newcastle Edinburgh and Direct Glasgow Railway.

The line via Kelso would have had less expenditure required because the Caledonian Railway Peebles branch would have been utilised, merely requiring similar upgrading along the lines of that already described for Alnwick-Cornhill. The route would have been shorter between London and Glasgow, and lessened the traffic generated from Alnmouth and south therefrom to Edinburgh and west of that city, including the main line terminus at Glasgow (Queen St),potentially to nil, thus benefiting both the North Eastern and Caledonian Railways. The latter, heavily dependent on the west coast partnership with the London and North Western Railway would have lost nothing, for any Glasgow traffic (and through traffic further north) would still have to run over its metals. It would have gained handsomely, however, by losing the heavy operating costs of through passenger and freight traffic over Beattock, always a thorn in its flesh. (There is the exact equivalent in road transport to-day, where we see many heavy goods vehicles from the South and Midlands of England, bound for Glasgow, using not the M1, M6 and A74 but M1,

AI, A66 and so to the A74.)

In sum, the 'East-coast' main line would have been: King's Cross, York, Newcastle, Alnwick, Kelso, Galashiels, Carstairs and so to Glasgow. Apart from the short start from King's Cross up to Finsbury park, the steepest gradient would have been to Stoke Summit in the Lincolnshire Wolds. This would have been very different to the West-Coast main line. Here the bank from Euston to Camden at the start exactly matched that from King's Cross to Finsbury Park, but thereafter there was Madely, Shap and Beattock Summits to be encountered.

But we have reached journey's end, for, tantalising as such possibilities are, we have now reached the realms of speculation rather than history.

References

References

REFERENCES

Railway Abbreviations used in this work

B.C.R	Border Counties Railway
B. & T.R	Blyth & Tyne Railway
B.U.R	Border Union Railway
C.E.R	Caledonian Extension Railway
C.N.R	Central Northumberland Railway
C.R	Caledonian Railway
E.& D.R	Edinburgh & Dalkeith Railway
E.& G.R	Edinburgh & Glasgow Railway
G.D.& C.R	Glasgow, Dumfries and Carlisle Railway
G.& S.W.R	Glasgow & South Western Railway
H.R	Hartlepool Railway
K.& S.G.R	Killingworth & Scots Gap Railway
L.& Y.R	Lancashire & Yorkshire Railway
L.& N.W.R	London & North Western Railway
M.H.& G.D.R	Manchester Hawick & Glasgow Direct Railway
M.R	Midland Railway
N.& B.R	Newcastle & Berwick Railway
N.& C.R	Newcastle & Carlisle Railway
N.D.& W.J.R	Newcastle Derwent & Weardale Junction Railway
N.E.& G.D.R	Newcastle Edinburgh & Glasgow Direct Railway
N.B.R	North British Railway
N.C.R	Northumberland Central Railway
N.E.R	North Eastern Railway
N.N.R	North Northumberland Railway
S.B.& B.R	Symington Biggar & Broughton Railway
S.& C.R	Settle & Carlisle Railway
S.D.& L.U.R	South Durham & Lancashire Union Railway
S.& D.R	Stockton & Darlington Railway
S.N.R	South Northumberland Railway
S.& S.G.R	Scotswood & Scots Gap Railway
W.R (W.V.R)	Wansbeck Valley Railway
Y.N.& B.R	York Newcastle & Berwick Railway

A Note on Place Names

Place names have been kept constant for the sake of simplicity and usually in their modern Ordnance Survey form e.g. Scots Gap has had a variety of spellings over the years.

Northumberland Central Railway: Directors 1863-72

Director	Description	Location of Estate	Residence
3rd Earl Grey	Aristocracy	Howick Hall	
Sir W.C.Trevelyan	Gentry	Hartburn Parish	Wallington Hall
Richard Hodgson-(Huntley)	Gentry	Near Cornhill	Carham Hall
Sir Horace St.Paul	Gentry	Wooler District	Ewart Park
George A.Grey	Estate Manager	Kirknewton (for Earl of Carlisle)	Milfield Hall
Sir Walter B.Riddell (London)	Gentry	Rothbury District	Non-resident
Thomas Gow	Land Agent	Cambo (for Trevelyan & Swinburn)	
Charles W.Ord	Gentry	Netherwitton	Nunnykirk
Henry Morton (Fencehouses)	Estate Manager	Wooler District (for Earl of Durham)	Non-resident
Sir John Swinburn Capheaton	Gentry		
John Hodgson-Hinde Newcastle	Gentry		
William Forster Jnr.	Farmer	Rothbury District	Rothbury
John Ord Non-resident (Kelso)	Esquire		
George Culley	Gentry	Wooler District	Fowberry Tower
John Bolam	Gentry	Alwinton	Alwinton

The next two pages contain comments on each of the Directors

References

Director	Comment
3rd Earl Grey	No obvious advantage to his estate from the N.C.R, but an early promoter of an east coast route. By his own statement he was merely acting "pro bono publicos". He proved a hard working Chairman.
Sir W.C.Trevelyan	A leading promoter of the N.C.R. Saw great potential for the improvement of his Estate through railways, particularly by the transport of lime. Was Chairman of the Wansbeck Railway.
Richard Hodgson (Huntley)	Sone of John Hodgson of Elswick Hall, Newcastle. He did not own an Estate but lived at Carham. A complex character, shrewd and capable of financial manipulation but hard working and able to hold down a variety of important posts e.g. M.P. for Berwick upon Tweed and later Tynemouth and even after his fall from power as Chairman of the North British Railway retained the post of High Sheriff of Northumberland.
Sir Horace St Paul	Came from a comparatively new family to Northumberland. His father is said to have removed himself as far as possible from London after a duelling incident. Had a genuine interest in Glendale and from his base at Ewart Park and supported the N.B.R and N.E.R according to which one would best serve the district. Thus he was Vice-chairman of the N.C.R and felt able to support N.E.R in 1880.
George A Grey	A capable and energetic businessman. Was early supporter of the N.C.R but anticipated trouble and resigned before the Bill was passed by Parliament (see Chapter 4). However his views altered and later he supported the Central Northumberland Railway scheme of 1880.
Sir W.B.Riddell	Resident of Hepple when in Northumberland and chaired Rothbury meetings. His principal residence was in London. He appeared late on the scene and does not appear to have had too great a grasp of railway affairs.
Thomas Gow	Sometime auditor to N.C.R.
Charles W Ord	Originator of plan to abandon north of Rothbury.
Henry Morton	Concientous manager of the Estates of the Earl of Durham. Steadfastly supported the railway and became a director of the N.C.R in 1880.

Sir John Swinburn   The doyen of Northumberland railway promoters. He acted on his own initiative to promote S & S.G.R. At first supported C.N.R in 1880 but retired when he saw the deteriorating financial situation.

J Hodgson-Hinde   Older half-brother of Richard Hodgson. He was a director of C.R. and had planned that railways take over of the N & C.R which failed. If his plan had come to fruition the railway situation between Tyne & Forth might have developed differently. He remained an active shareholder in the N.C.R.

William Forster   From an early date a keen supporter of the 'through central' route policy from 1863 to 1881.

John Ord   The only director from north of The Border, where he was a keen supporter of the 'through central route' policy in areas including Coldstream, Kelso and Melrose.

George Culley   An energetic land-improver following on the work of his father. He might have promoted 'local agricultural lines' if the original N.C.R scheme had been completed and he had the opportunities for this.

John Bolam   An early supporter of railways in the Coquet valley and of the N.C.R.. d.1866.

1.   U.N.L. Trevelyan Mss, WCT 304, Copy of Shareholders Address Book of the Northumberland Central Railway corrected up to 1st December 1868, pursuant to section 34 of Regulation of Railways Act 1868.

2.   Ibid, Various N.C.R half yearly reports.

From: Moore D.W. MA thesis (Unpup) Newcastle 1984 with additional material by the Author.

References

CHAPTER 1.

1. The Railway Magazine. Jan. 1917. Article by R Lendrum-Ainslie.

2.e.g. Sewell G.W.M. The North British Railway in Northumberland. Merlin .Devon.(1991); Jenkins.S.C. The Rothbury Branch, Oakwood Press (1991).

3.For an overview see; Lewis. M.J.T Early Wooden Railways. Routledge, Keegan and Paul. London. (1970); Baxter. B.Stone Blocks and Iron Rails. David & Charles Newton Abbott (1966).; Lee C.E The Evolution of Railways, parts III & VIII. The Railway Gazette. London (1943).
4. For the classic description see (Dendy) Marshall C.F. A History of British Railways Down to the Year 1830 O.U.P. (1938). Ch. II The North of England & VI Scotland (including The Edinburgh & Dalkeith.)

5. Thus the Swinburnes of Capheaton, The Trevelyans of Wallington and St Paul of Ewart Park, for example, have prominent roles in events. An undated letter in the Trevelyan papers (Robinson Library, U.N.L), clearly written in the early 1860's lists prominent shareholders as: Carr-Ellison 200; W.Selby 100: Lord Lambton 50; Arthur Middleton Bart 50; Sir John Swinburne Bt 50; Trevelyan was indicated as absent abroad (see text); minor shareholders (10 or less) of interest included Mr Hughes of Middleton Hall, John Robinson Esq. of Rosenworth Cottage, Gosforth; and so on down to Archdeacon Hamilton who had one.

6. Warn.C.R Waggonways and Early Railways of Northumberland; The Railways of the Northumberland Coalfield. Frank Graham. Newcastle upon Tyne (1976); Davidson M.F The Blyth & Tyne Railway.pt 1. Etal (1990) .Wells J.A The Blyth & Tyne Branch. N.R.O (1990).

7. The Tranent & Cockenzie Waggonway is frequently mentioned by historians of the rebellion of 1745.. For a railway historians view see Lee.C.E op. cit.p.83.

8. Thomas J. The North British Railway Vol 1. (1969); Dow.G. The First Railway across The Border. L.N.E.R (1946).

9. see, for example, Whittle G. The Newcastle & Carlisle Railway. David & Charles, Newton Abbott.

10. Ferguson. N. The True Line Vol. 12. p 42.; Mulley. A.J. Rails across The Border. Patrick Stephens. Wellingborough. (1990).

11. This is of course a generalisation with exceptions. For example, in 1871 The General Manager of the N.E.R had to be dismissed. see Simmons J. The Express Train and Other Stories. David St John Pub'd (1994). Also in Tomlinson's W.W The North Eastern Railway. It's Rise and Development 1st ed. 1914.

12. Again a generalisation. There would be many diligent officers working for the N.B.R The matter is dealt with in detail in Thomas J. op. cit.

13. Northumberland Central Railway Act (26 & 27) Vic. Cap 335. 28.07.65; Northumberland Central Railway Act (V9c. 30-31 Cap 9) 12.04.67; North British & Northumberland Central Railway Amalgamation Act (Vic 35.&36. Cap 192) August 1874.

14. Moore D.W. The Promotion and Extension of Railways in Central Northumberland 1850-1886. p.167. unpub. M.A. thesis, U.N.L.; Sewell.G.W.M. op. cit. p.82.

15. For example, see Trevelyan and Hodgson, both quoted below. Minutes of N.B.R in S.R.O.

16. For example, the Newton on the Moor overhead bucket line to Brinkburn was extended across the A1 trunk road in order to lead coal from the Whittle/Shilbottle colliery complex when these were split. (the author is grateful to Mr J. Lilley of Whittingham for directing his attention to this.). Another example is excursion traffic from Kelso promoted by the N.E.R The N.B.R and N.C.R might have tapped this traffic.

CHAPTER 2.

1. For a fuller account see Dow.G. Op. Cit.; Thomas J. op. cit; Tomlinson.W.W op. cit; Warn. C.R. Main Line Railways of Northumberland. Frank Graham (Newcastle upon Tyne) (1976); However, the earliest proposal of 1835 was virtually an unsuccessful copy of the Blyth & Tyne Railway i.e. an amalgamation of colliery waggonways. At least one proposal was purely Edinburgh based.

2. Moore. D.W op.cit. Table 1. p.11 The outcome was a compromise between local proposals and Hudson-inspired schemes from the south.

3 B.P.P. 1841, xii p. 79, quoted and commented upon by Moore D.W.,op. cit.. This work also has a brief account of the part played by Bowman.

4. Accepted waggonway practice continued into the railway era is a debated subject For example, even The Stockton & Darlington Railway, dubiously quoted as "the first public railway" had rope-worked inclines and horse drawn passenger services. The Kelso, Melrose and Dalkeith Waggonway of 1817-20 was associated with the Roxburgh and Selkirk Tramway, demonstrating the lengthening of routes before the railway age. See. Mullay A.J op. cit. and Thomas. J. op. cit.

5. Of necessity this is the essence of a complicated episode in the political history of railways. Fuller details will be found in many works including those of Moore, Mulley and Tomlinson quoted above.

6. U.N.L. WCT MSS 2296 contains an undated newspaper cutting pasted into a Trevelyan scrapbook. It indicates that the N.E & G.D.R was of more than passing interest to Trevelyan and to that most enthusiastic of railway promoting landowners, Sir John Swinburne. The cutting reads as follows;-

References

At the meeting of landowners on or near the line of railway proposed to be made by a company calling itself The Newcastle-upon-Tyne, Edinburgh and Direct Glasgow Railway, with a branch to Hexham, having considered the proposed line, and explained with Mr Monck, The Chairman of the managing committee of the said railway company, are of the opinion that the proposed line of railway, both in its main line of country through which it will pass, and to our estates, in affording the shortest and easiest communication between Glasgow, Edinburgh and Newcastle-upon-Tyne and in opening out to use the lime and other minerals which may be now lying in our lands, we are of the opinion, therefore, that the projectors of the proposed line ought to have our consent and support, subject to all such reservations, in regard to all private and personal interests as is usual in such cases.

Belsay Castle Inn. November 10th 1845. Signed;
John E. Swinburne, John Forster. W.D. Dent. P.G. Ellison (for Ralph Bates Esq.). J.S Ogle. Chas M.L. Monck, Thomas James. R.C.Askew (for self and the Misses Davidson). Thomas Anderson, Thomas Atkinson, Harle.

7. Newcastle Journal. 1846-77. On 29.8.46. the half-yearly meeting of the N.B.R voted in favour of £600,000 to upgrade the Edinburgh & Leith branch, to extend the Haddington and Kelso branches to those towns and some shares to go to existing shareholders in the Edinburgh & Perth Railway. This illustrates the wildly extravagant nature of railway investment at the time. The Newcastle Journal was strongly pro-Hudson and anti-N.B.R particularly taking the opportunity of the flood damage (reported on 30.10.46 et sub.) to attack the N.B.R. (McCord N. pers. comm. with quotes and comments).

8. Thomas J. op. cit. Vol. 1 p.67.

9. For Caledonian Railway expansion schemes and financial troubles see, for example, Nock.O.S. The Caledonian Railway (London) Ian Allan 1973 p.29-35. Murray commenting on the "wild finances" of the time cites the C.R as raising £380,000 capital for construction of the main line, which it promptly invested in other companies, hence the inability to buy out The Newcastle & Carlisle and The Edinburgh & Glasgow Rlys.

10.The independently promoted Edinburgh & Dunbar Railway failed. In 1846 Hudson offered to lease the N.B.R at 8%. The N.B.R reacted to such threats by active promotional schemes south of The Border. see. Thomas. J. op. cit. p.83.

11. For the components of the Glasgow & South Western Rly see, for example, "The Glasgow & Sourth Western Railway" pub. Stephenson Locomotive Society 1950. ch.1

12. For Mullay's full exposition see. Mullay A.J. op. cit. p.36. Also for his comments on the "North British Triangle" (Edinburgh-Berwick-Carlisle) and routes south of Edinburgh (Waverley). For the Symington, Biggar and Broughton line see Thomas. J. op.cit; Regional History of Great Britain Vol 6, Rev. Peterson (David & Charles) 1984 p. 152.

13.For Tyne & Edinburgh proposal see 6 above.

14. The N. & C.R North Tyne proposal was known as The Great North of England Junction Railway initially (a significant title); later the Darlington & Hawick Junction Railway adopted much of the route in 1846. The former utilised the North Tyne valley and the latter included the Wear Valley extension plan. [P.R.O Kew. 509/17; Railway Gazette No 29 Vol 1. 1st Oct 1845. p.493.].

15. Tomlinson. W.W. op. cit.

CHAPTER 3.

1. Warn.C.R Railways of the Northumberland Coalfield (Newcastle- upon-Tyne) 1976. p.10-1

2. Fenwick. H.A.C,. Brinkburn. Pers. Comm. re iron working at Brinkburn to whom the author is grateful. Sewell G.W.M. op. cit. p. 79.gives without stating sources that the expectation of fall of price of lime in Morpeth was to 5/- per ton- a 30% drop.

3. Mullay. A.J. op. cit. p.63. Newcastle Chronicle 05.11.1852; 03.06.1853. U.N.L Trev. M.S.S WCT304

4.Sewell. G.W.M. op. cit. p.11. For a more detailed description of events see Tomlinson op. cit; Nock O.S.Scottish Railways (Nelson) 1950.

5. J.F. Tone was a remarkably active professional civil engineer, very much a Northumbrian, although he worked elsewhere e.g. in the West Country. He began his career on the Newcastle and North Shields Railway, became a partner in his uncle's business (Nicholson & Tone) and continued in sole charge after Nicholson's death. Besides railway engineering he had other interests including that of managing director of the Hareshaw Ironworks, Bellingham and co-ownership of Plashetts Colliery. He had two faults. Whilst he had his supporters he easily made enemies and he tended to under-estimate costs. Sewell pers comm.

6. S.R.O BR/NBR/1/9 Minutes of the N.B.R meeting on 14.10.1859 for Hexham Darlington & Hartlepool contact. N.R.O Armstrong MSS 309/D6 for the Hexham & Skipton Railway proposal. Also letters with reference to meetings between Tone, Hodgson, Beaumont and T. Bewick, quoted in Moore. D.W op. cit. p.50. This important reference appears to have otherwise gone unrecorded.

7. Sewell. G.W.M. op. cit. p. 79.

8. U.N.L Trev. M.S.S. WCT 304, The Morpeth & Rothbury Railway.

9. Moore. D.W op. cit. p. 139.

10. Sewell. G.M.W op. cit. p.19. Wansbeck Railway Act 08.08.59 (22 & 23 Vic. Cap 125)

References

11. Warn. C.R. Rural Branch Lines in Northumberland p. 28.

12. U.N.L. Trev. M.S.S 301, correspondence between Woodman & Trevelyan.

13. ibid. letter to subscribers 14.09.1858; S.R.O BR/WBR/2.

14. N.R.O. Woodman MSS ZAN/M6/3/3. Morperth Collectinea Vol. 3 p.130

15. Sewell G.W.B op. cit. p. 79-81 gives a fuller and excellent account; see also Thornthwaite. Archaeologica Aeliana Fifth series Vol xix p.100-4.

16. Sewell. G.W.M. op. cit. p.81; U.N.L. Trev. MSS WCT 304.

17. Thomas J. op. cit. p.114.

18. Vallance H.A. Border Counties Railway; Railway Magazine Sept 1955.

19. Mullay. op. cit. p.5 comments on B.C.R speeds if built to standard of the Settle & Carlisle.

20. Thomas. J. op. cit. p.116.

21. ibid. p.121.

22. Tomlinson op. cit. p. 850 et sub; U.N.L Trev. M.S.S WCT 304.

23. Davidson M.F. Blyth & Tyne Railway. Vol 1 pp 16-18; Warn C.R Railways of the Northumberland Coalfield pp 11.14,17.

CHAPTER 4.

1. "The Northumberland Village Book". Northumberland Federation of Women's Institutes (1994). p. 559 and Potts Mrs P. pers. comm.

2. U.N.L Trev. MSS WCT 301. Minutes of Morpeth meeting. 22.11.59.

3. U.N.L.Trev. MSS WCT 278. Minutes of Morpeth meeting 22.11.59.

4. U.N.L Trev MSS WCT 304. Minutes of Morpeth meeting 1863. Confusion sometimes occurs between the titles Northumberland Central Railway and Central Northumberland Railway. This arose partly because at the time some people had the concept of the "through-central route" very much in mind rather than a local railway - thus at an early age "Central" was a stressed word for some. The title C.N.R was thus used widely after this meeting until the change of title was made in the Bill of 1863 and subsequent Act. This is made clear by PRO (8) 1/1/23 in the S.R.O which states; "[The] Central Northumberland Railway from Scots Gap to Coldstream was incorporated in 1863 with the title Northumberland Central Railway" The title Central Northumberland Railway re-emerges in 1880.

5. Sewell. G.W.M op. cit. p.82.

6. Warn. op. cit. p. 30. U.N.L. Trev. MSS 302.

7. P.R.O Rail 527/1745 quoted and discussed by Moore D.W opp. cit. p. 60. Report by John and Thomas Thompson on proposed railway 12.17.60.

8. ibid.

9. Moore D.W op. cit. p.15 table 2.

10 U.N.L. Trev. MSS WCT 301.

11. Alnwick Mercury. 01.04.1862.

12.ibid.

13. ibid.

14. Sewell.G.W.M op. cit. p. 82 & pers. comm.; Flatman B. Northumberland Railway Branch Lines (Alnwick) undated. The last paragraph om p.1 contains interesting observations but clearly must refer to the N.C.R not the C.N.R.

15. Sewell.G.W.M ibid.

16. Jenkins S.C The Rothbury Branch. (Oakwood Press) 1991 .p. 14.

17. ibid.

18. Moore D.W op. cit. p. 159 et sub; correspondence between Woodman and Earl Grey.

19. Gateshead Observer. Oct 14th 1847 signed "a traveller".

20. Moore. D.W ibid.

21 Summary of Northumberland Central Railway Act. N.R.O 162 AN M 16/b; N.R.O 2BU D4; S.R.O N.C.R 1.1.11.

CHAPTER 5.

1. Sewell. G.W.M op. cit. p.83 and pers. comm.

2. Northern Daily Express 12.08.64; Newcastle Daily Journal, same date.

3. Jenkins S.C. op. cit. p.17

4. U.N.L Trev. MSS WCT 304.

References

5. AC 4th Duke of Northumberland (Misc Letters) Vol. 14 p.82, as reported by Moore.

6. U.N.L. Trev. MSS WCT 304

7. Moore D.W op. cit. p.168.

8. U.N.L Trev. MSS WCT 304

9. ibid; Sewell G.W.M op. cit.

10. Letter Benjamin Woodman to Earl Grey '14.03.1865.

11. Jenkins op. cit. p.22

12 ibid p.22-3.

CHAPTER 6.

1.N.R.O 855 Box 2. For greater detail see Cottrell P.L "Railway Finance in the Crisis of 1866". Journal of Transport History, new series vol iii (1975-6).

2. For greater detail see Baker & Savage. "The Economic History of Transport".

3. Chambers W. "About Railways" 1856 p.19.

4. For a full ,account see. S.H.S Series IV 1978. "The North British Railway Enquiry of 1866, ed. Vamplew. W.

5. U.N.L Trev. MSS Txt WCT various letters

6. U.N.L. Trev. MSS WCT 22; Sewell G.W.M. pers. comm.

7. ibid.

8. Moore D.W op. cit. p.173; Sewell G.W.M op. cit. p. 83; Jenkins S.C op. cit. p. 26; U.N.L Trev MSS WCT 304. AC 5th Duke of Northumberland letters Vol 2 p.231 reported by Moore.

9. U.N.L Trev. MSS WCT 22; N.R.O Swinburne MSS 2SW/C 60.

10.ibid.

11. N.R.O 322/B

12. AC 6th Duke of Northumberland. Misc letters 1869-70 Vol 2 p.22 reported by Moore; U.N.L Trev. MSS WCT 22; Report N.C.R Director's Meeting 18.12.66. The Duke required as a condition of funding a through-central route from Newcastle to Scotland (Kelso). The B.C.R, W.R and B & T.R. route was clearly considered insufficient.

13. U.N.L Trev. MSS WCT 22 & 304.

14. Moore D.W. op. cit. pp 172-4.

15. U.N.L trev. MSS WCT 304.

16. Jenkins S.C op. cit. pp 26-28; Sewell G.W.M pers. comm.

17. ibid (but see later Hodgson letter of 23.07.71 to Newcastle Daily Chronicle.)

18. Jenkins S.C op. cit. p.27; Sewell G.W.M pers. comm.

19. U.N.L Trev. MSS WCt 304.

20. Moore D.W op. cit. p.174. Report half-yearly meeting of 7th February 1868, Capital account to 31.12.67; report half-yearly meeting July 1868; Newcastle Daily Journal 30th Sept. 1867 for N.C.R extra-ordinary general meeting of 31st August 1867.

21. Phillips. A. A History of Banks, Bankers and Banking in Northumberland p.250 quoted by Moore.

22. For the full Board of Trade Inspectors report see Jenkins. S.C op. cit. pp 31-2.

23. Lynn R.W and Sewell G.W.M "A Serious Accident on the Northumberland Central Railway" (unpub).

24. Jenkins S.C. op. cit. p.31-2.

25. For a full account see Sewell G.W.M op. cit. p.101 and 108-13.

26. Newcastle Daily Chronicle. 10.06.71 for letter from G.A Grey; and correspondence 26th August 71 et. sub.

CHAPTER 7.

1. Sewell. G.W.M op. cit. p. 81.

2.U.N.L Trev. MSS. N.C.R half-yearly report 26.02.71.

3. Sewell G.W.M op. cit. p. 85.

4. ibid.

5. Moore D.W op. cit p 177

6. U.N.L Trev. MSS WCT 304.

7. U.N.L Trev. MSS WCT 303.

References

8. Sewell. G.W.M op. cit. Sewell draws attention to the fact that Tone continually under-estimated expenses and could be hopelessly out. This caused problems when he was engineer to other projects e.g. The Border Counties Railway where the capital employed was £250,000. Tone thought initially that it could be built for £200,000 and later reduced this to £180,000.

9. Moore D.W op. cit. p. 179.

10. S.R.O BR/PYB/ 314.

11. Sewell G.W.M op. cit. p.85.

12. Moore D.W op.cit p. 179.

CHAPTER 8.

1. The Blyth & Tyne (Newcastle Extension Act).

2. Warn C.R Railways of the Northumberland Coalfield pp17,29 (Newcastle) Graham.F.1976.

3. Davidson M.F Blyth & Tyne Railway; part 1 p. 21.

4. Moore. D.W op. cit. p.67

5. ibid p. 67 & 69.

6 ibid. p. 68

7. ibid.

8. Warn. op. cit. p. 29.

9. NRO Swinburne MSS ZSW 322/8/

10. BPP 1882 xxii

11. P.R.O Rail 527/1744 (2).

CHAPTER 9.

1. Newcastle Daily Journal 1st March 1867.

2. Moore D.W op. cit. p. 168

3. ibid.

4. Irving. North Eastern Railway 1870-1914 .p.28.

5. Jenkins. S.C op. cit. p.45-6.

6. ibid. p. 46.

7. Wooler & Kelso Railway. Lundie & Lundie (Cardiff) 1881.

CHAPTER 10.

1.e.g. Tomlinson. op. cit.; Warn op. cit; Stobbs Memories of the L.N.E.R in Rural Northumberland p. 11 pub. privately (Penrith) 1986.

2. Newcastle Daily Journal 23rd Jan. 1881. Editorial.

3.Stephens. R.M secretary, Stephenson Locomotive Society, Newcastle-upon-Tyne. pers. comm.

4. see, for example, Thompson H. Highways and Byways of Northumberland. Macmillan (London) 1921 p.314.

5. Armstrong P. Whittingham. Weatherburn J.(Whittingham). pers. comm. based on Northumberland Village Book under Netherton.

6. e.g. Tomlinson op. cit; Warn C.R Rural Branch Lines of Northumberland; Stobbs A.W op. cit.Flatman B. op. cit.

7. P.R.O Rail 527/1745 Plans, Reports, Traffic Tables for the Alnwick-Cornhill branch, including report by the Alnwick Railway Committee, July 1860 and survey of a railway and branches by Thompson, including Rothbury branch.; Alnwick Mercury 10th Oct 1861; P.R.O Rail/5277/10 for Dickson's later and final attempt.

8. Flatman D. op. cit p. 1.; Alnwick Mercury 10th Oct 1864; U.N.L Trev. MSS WCT 304 for St Pauls change of view to favour the N.C.R at the promotion meeting Feb. 1863.

9. Newcastle Daily Chronicle. 24th Dec 1880 and subsequent correspondence.

10. Wilson "Notes on Northern Farms and Farming" p.5 et sub.

11. Newcastle Daily Chronicle '14th Feb. 1881; N.R.O Swinburne MSS ZSW 322/B/add; ; ZSW 322/B/51; Newcastle Daily Journal 23rd Jan. 1881.

12. N.R.O Swinburne MSS ZSW/B/51; Kelso Chronicle.

13. N.R.O Swinburne MSS ZSW/B/add (iii).

14. ibid; Newcastle Daily Chronicle 20th Dec 1881.

15. Moore D.W op. cit. p. 84.

References

16. S.R O PYB/314.

17. N.R.O Swinburne MSS ZSW/B/51.

18. Flatman B. op. cit. p.2 These figures must surely be incorrect, perhaps estimates. Confirmation is not possible in the absence of references. Flatman gives an excellent summary of the situation.

19. U.N.L Trev. MSS WCT 304.

20. S .R.O N.C.R N. H4.

21. ibid.; N.R.O (16)M; U.N.L Trev. MSS WCT 304.

22. U.N.L Trev. MSS WCT 304; BPP 1882 xxii.

23. Moore D.W op. cit. pp 83-5

24. Moore D.W ibid.

25. N.R.O Swinburne MSS 23 W322/B/51.

26. Brown M. Records & Recollections (Journal of Aln & Breamish Local History Society)

27. Moore. D.W op. cit. p 255.

28. ibid p.256.

CHAPTER 11.

1. S.R.O/BR/NBR/8/1209.

2. P.R.O Rail 527/1665.

3. Petrie J. Pers. Comm.

4. Armstrong. W. (Whittingham) pers. comm.

5. Flatman op. cit. p.7. This work has good photographs of station architecture.

6. Petrie. J. pers. comm.

7. This may not be nearly as fanciful as it first appears. Charles Forman of Forman & McCall Ltd of Glasgow, born in 1852, was a man of great experience in railway construction, some overseas, but much in the West of Scotland e.g. The Glasgow Central Railway. One project which was surveyed by him but did not come to fruition was The Glasgow, Berwick & Newcastle Direct Railway (see Thomas J. The West Highland Railway p.49 (Pan Books) 1970.

—A—
Acklington and Rothbury Railway, 23, 140
Alnwick Board of Health, 41, 43, 135
Alnwick faction, 41, 45, 134, 143
Alnwick-Cornhill Railway, 42, 44, 129, 133, 145, 150, 162
Armsrong, Sir W, 140, 142
Auger, Rev Dr, 140, 143
—B—
B & T.R, 6,21, 23, 30, 56, 104, 111, 114
Bank Charter Act, 81
Blyth and Tyne Railway Act, 9
Border Counties Railway, 18, 21, 26, 30, 60, 77, 96, 104, 121
Border Counties Railway Act (North Tyne Section), 27
Border Union Railway, 10, 21, 25, 27, 30, 33
Border, The, 10, 14, 18, 21, 26, 30, 55, 81, 124
Boulton Trowsdale & Son, 59
Bradshaw's Shareholders Manual, 97
British Parliamentary papers, 117
Bruce, George, 60,92,94,et sub
Brunlees, J, 138, 148
Buccleugh, Duke of, 148
—C—
Cadogan, W, 23, 27
Caledonian Extension Railway, 19
Carr, Ralph of Hedgeley, 40, 46, 50
Carr-Ellison, Captain, 135, 149
Carr-Ellison, Ralph, 60, 77, 149, 187
Central north-south routes, 18
Central Northumberland Railway, 129, 134, 150, 151, 154,
Central openings, 21
Central routes, 16, 19, 26, 42, 45, 102, 122, 137, 144, 159
Charlton, W.H. of Hesleyside, 26
Cockermouth, Keswick and Penrith Railway, 57
Core Railway, 154, 155
Court of Chancery, 48, 64, 110
Culley, George, 51, 59, 61
—D—
Dickson, J of Saughton, 47
Dickson, William, 41, 42
Dowson, 77, 78, 87, 95
—E—
E & G.R, 16, 18, 32, 33
Earl Grey, 39, 47, 50, 55, 59, 75, 89, 91, 93, 101, 150
Edinburgh & Dalkeith Railway, 7, 14, 15, 25
Eliot of Clifton Park, 144, 145, 146
Enclosure Commissioners, 47, 48
Ewesley Station, 98, 108

Index

Index

Dedicated to the Memory
of
Catherine Mackichan

Design & Illustration by J.Hutchinson
Text Origination by George Skipper
Maps by John Rayner of Harbottle Information Technology

Published by
N.D.Mackichan, Aros, Whittingham, Alnwick, Northumberland NE66 4RF

ISBN No: 0 953127702